DCC
PROJECTS & APPLICATIONS
— VOLUME 3 —

Mike Polsgrove
with
Cody Grivno

KALMBACH BOOKS

About the authors
Mike Polsgrove

Mike Polsgrove wrote *Model Railroader* magazine's "DCC Corner" column from 2003 to 2014. He has a Bachelor of Science degree in electrical engineering from the Milwaukee School of Engineering and has worked as the motive power electrical engineer for two prototype railroads. Since 1989 he has been designing digital electronic circuits for Eagle Test Systems.

Mike has been a model railroader since the 1960s, and he is currently building his fourth layout, an HO scale railroad depicting the Soo Line's Third Subdivision of the Eastern Division, circa 1963. *DCC Projects and Applications Vol. 3* is his third book.

Cody Grivno

Cody Grivno is an associate editor for *Model Railroader* magazine, and also serves as the host of the popular "Cody's Workshop" video segment on Model Railroader Video Plus (ModelRailroader.com). The Minnesota native enjoys many facets of model railroading, and plans on modeling the Minnesota Northern Warroad Sub in HO scale. He lives in the Milwaukee area with his wife, Dorothy, and two children.

Kalmbach Books
21027 Crossroads Circle
Waukesha, Wisconsin 53186
www.Kalmbach.com/Books

Published in 2015
19 18 17 16 15   1 2 3 4 5

ISBN: 978-0-89024-982-6
EISBN: 978-0-89024-983-3

Book Editor: Jeff Wilson
Book Design: Tom Ford

Unless noted, photographs were taken by the author.

The material in this book has previously appeared as articles in *Model Railroader* magazine. The articles have been edited to reflect current manufacturer information and products as much as possible, but may occasionally reference past magazine issues or products no longer available.

This product is a Print on Demand format of the original book published by Kalmbach Publishing Company.

Publisher's Cataloging-In-Publication Data

Polsgrove, Mike.
   DCC projects & applications / Mike Polsgrove with Cody Grivno
   v. : ill. ; cm. -- (Model railroader books)

   "The material in this book has previously appeared as articles in Model railroader magazine."--T.p. verso
   ISBN: 0-89024-645-9 (v. 1)
   ISBN: 978-0-89024-774-7 (v. 2)
   ISBN: 978-0-89024-982-6 (v. 3)

1. Digital Control Systems. 2. Railroads--Models. 3. Railroads--Models--Design and Construction. I. Grivno, Cody. II. Title: Digital command control projects & applications

TF197 .P67 2006
625.1/9

Contents

Introduction

Welcome to *DCC Projects & Applications Vol. 3*, the third book in Mike Polsgrove's series on Digital Command Control. While some aspects of DCC have stayed the same since *DCC Projects & Applications Vol. 2* in 2010, much has also changed. This book features a new lineup of stories and updated tips and techniques.

To catch up on the latest innovations and projects in the marketplace, look below to read Mike's two-page report on what's new in DCC. Learn about new stationary, motor, and sound decoders; control systems; throttles; and website updates, among other items.

If you're unsure about making the switch from direct current to DCC, check out Chapter 1. There, you'll get an explanation of what DCC is, some basic terminology, the tools you need to install decoders, and solutions for short circuits.

For those of you planning to convert your DC layout to DCC, flip over to Chapter 2 and read the 10 tips for converting a model railroad to DCC. Also in that chapter, you'll learn how to calculate power for a DCC system, install track buses, wire reverse sections, update older DCC systems, and more.

Installing and programming decoders are areas where modelers often struggle. After reading Chapters 3 and 4, these tasks should become much easier. First, in Chapter 3, we'll look at 10 decoder installs. Have an N scale diesel that needs a decoder? See pages 38 and 46. Want to bring that old Athearn HO locomotive into the digital age? See pages 44 and 72.

Once you have the decoder installed, go to Chapter 4 to learn a variety of programming tips. Mike will explain what configuration variables are; share basic programming tips; and demonstrate how to speed match different locomotives, add momentum, and build a consist.

If you believe that your models should be seen *and* heard, then Chapter 5 is just for you. After reading a primer on how sound decoders work, check out four how-to stories on sound decoder installations. Many of the tips covered in those articles can be used for your next sound install.

Finally, we'll wrap things up with seven stories about lighting and DCC. Headlights are just the tip of the iceburg with DCC. With digital technology, you can enjoy models with working rotary beacons, Mars lights, ditch lights, classification lights, and more. Throttle-controlled passenger car lighting is also possible with DCC, as covered on page 84. For the ultimate in cool lighting effects, read about controlling a train-order signal on page 86.

There are a lot of possibilities with DCC. Whether you want to install a motor decoder in your favorite locomotive or you want your engine to have prototypical sound, light, and momentum effects, there is something for all skill levels in this book. Good luck on your next DCC project!

What's new in DCC

Here's an update on some of the latest innovations and products to enter the Digital Command (DCC) marketplace.

The ability to update DCC software or firmware without sending it back to the manufacturer is a feature many companies have been adding to their products. Updating products by physically changing EEPROMs (Electrically Erasable Programmable Read-Only Memories) that contain firmware has been available since the dawn of DCC. Today's methods involve downloading firmware from the Internet and using a computer and special hardware to then download it directly into the product.

Keeping trains running over dirty track is another advancement many companies have been working on. This usually involves installing an additional module that's wired into the decoder, but some newer decoders have the feature built in.

Let's take a look at some company-specific products.

CVP has refined its AD4 stationary decoder. Improvements include easier setup, a redesigned circuit to work better with newer DCC systems, and redesigned input circuitry that can be used with higher-voltage (large scale) DCC systems.

The company also released its T5000E wireless throttle, featuring an accessory decoder mode, adjustable transmitter power, and eight-slot locomotive memory.

For Z scalers, Digitrax offers the UP6Z, which is really two products in one. The primary function is to reduce DCC track voltage by 4-6 volts so it's usable for Z scale layouts. The other function is an expansion port for LocoNet. Each function is independent.

Digitrax continues to add to its line

of Z scale plug-and-play decoder board replacements for American Z Line and Märklin locomotives.

ESU released a large version of its LokSound sound decoder, the LokSoundXL V4.0. It's intended for O scale and larger locomotives.

The company is continually adding downloadable sound projects for its LokSound Select series of sound decoders, as well as updates to the software for its LokSound Programmer.

ESU also has the PowerPack module to keep its LokPilot V4.0 and LokSound V4.0 decoders running over dirty track.

Model Rectifier Corp. is adding to its Preferred Sound 16-bit sound decoder line. The firm also announced the Prodigy Elite DCC control system for large layouts. Unlike other Prodigy systems, the ProElite has a large display on the command station/booster that's capable of showing output voltage, current load, or a fast clock. It features 8-plus amps of output and allows simultaneous use of 99 cabs. It has two front-mounted cab jacks, one rear-mounted jack for booster output, and one rear-mounted jack for extra cabs, extension plates, wireless receiver, or PC interface.

NCE Corp. released its CAB06 line of throttles. These are basic throttles similar to the CAB04 but with an LED display. They're offered in radio and tethered versions.

NCE has also introduced the DCC Twin starter set. This system has two throttles built into the command station and an expansion port that allows the addition of six other NCE walkaround throttles like the Pro Cab, Power Cab, or any of the CAB0 (4, 5, or 6)-series throttles, plus three other devices such as its USB computer interface, the AIU (auxiliary input unit), or the Mini-Panel.

NCE's method of keeping a locomotive running over dirty track is the "No Halt Insurance" module. It allows a typical HO scale locomotive to travel over a stretch of dirty track up to 3 feet long without the lights flickering.

QSI Solutions has released a number of large-scale versions of its Titan sound decoder. The firm also has a

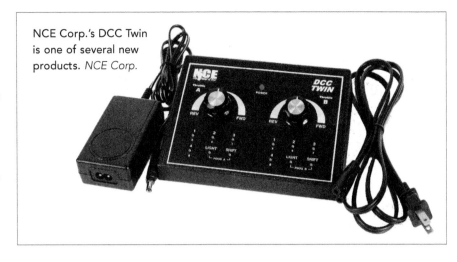

NCE Corp.'s DCC Twin is one of several new products. *NCE Corp.*

major firmware update for the Titan line called Emulation Technology. The upgrade improves the fidelity of the sound, motor control, and functionality. *Model Railroader* subscribers can see video of the Emulation Technology in action in part 1 of the 2012 National Train Show report.

SoundTraxx offers SurroundTraxx, an alternative to installing a sound decoder inside the locomotive. The device sends sounds to a series of wayside speakers that follow a locomotive around the layout.

The system uses feedback from Digitrax transponding decoders to determine the locomotive's location and sends the sound to the appropriate speaker. At this time a Digitrax command station, block occupancy detectors, and transponder detectors are required. The firm plans on developing systems for use with other DCC systems. You can learn more about the SurroundTraxx system in the March 2014 issue of *Model Railroader*.

SoundTraxx is adding to its popular Tsunami line of sound decoders. This includes new plug-and-play styles, such as the TSU-BA4000 for large-scale Bachmann Spectrum steam engines, and new sounds, including a supercharged Alco 251C and turbocharged Electro-Motive Division 567D prime movers.

Train Control Systems (TCS) is entering the sound decoder market with its WOWSound line of decoders. The first decoders are heavy, medium, and light steam. The company plans on making sound decoders that are

capable of downloading new sounds and maintaining a sound library on its website.

To keep trains running over dirty track, TCS offers various Keep Alive modules. It's also introducing new decoders with Keep Alive built in.

For many years, TCS has offered decoders with built-in 1.5V voltage regulators for use with light bulbs. Now it's adding LED current-limiting resistors, eliminating the need for external resistors.

Traintek LLC, traditionally a reseller of DCC and model railroad products, has introduced two new products. The first is the Aux-Box, a type of accessory decoder. Instead of outputting a voltage to control a turnout or other wayside device, the Aux-Box allows you to close (or open) eight 3-amp solid state switches. It also has two photocell inputs; the outputs can be programmed to flash.

The Aux-Box HC has four additional 8-amp switches. It can be used to turn on (or off) just about anything on a layout, including DCC track power in sections, such as a roundhouse or staging yard.

The second product is the Adapt-A-Board. It's available for more than a half dozen USA Trains large scale diesel locomotives. A large-scale DCC decoder plugs into the Adapt-A-Board, allowing for easy conversion to DCC. Some Adapt-A-Boards also include an LED lighting kit.

As you can see, the DCC marketplace continues to grow with new technologies and products.

Understanding Digital Command Control

It may seem hard to believe, but Digital Command Control (DCC) has been a prominent part of model railroading for nearly two decades. During this time, many people have made the switch from direct current (DC) to DCC to enjoy the many benefits that digital technology has to offer, such as running multiple engines on the same track, adding sound to locomotives and freight cars, and much more.

While many have made the switch, others are still on the fence about DCC. Because of this, manufacturers have strived to make DCC more user-friendly.

Starter systems (many of which can be expanded to grow with a model railroad), drop-in decoders, and models with factory-installed motor and sound decoders have made DCC accessible to hobbyists of all skill levels.

In this chapter, we'll take a look at what DCC is, commonly used terms and their definitions, the tools you'll need to get started installing decoders, and solutions for short circuits. Once you have a grasp of the basics, you'll be ready to start enjoying the benefits of DCC.

What is DCC?

Digital Command Control (DCC) has become a major part of the hobby over the past 15 years. In this relatively short amount of time, dozens of companies have produced hundreds of products that have enhanced the realism and operation of our layouts. For those of you new to command control, let's take a look at what DCC is and how it works.

The goal of any command control system is to operate more than one train at a time on the same track. Traditional DC control requires dividing your railroad into blocks. Each block is connected through a selector switch that can be set for one of two or more power packs. As a train moves across the railroad, each block has to be switched to the power pack controlling that train. The train's speed is controlled by the voltage and the direction by the polarity.

With DCC, operating information is sent through the rails in packets of high and low pulses representing binary code. By using digital signals, a variety of commands can be sent to a locomotive's decoder. This allows for independent control of movement as well as sounds and lights.

Much of DCC's success can be attributed to the development of stan-

Ditch lights are among the many effects that can be operated with Digital Command Control.

dards by the National Model Railroad Association (NMRA). This allows components from various manufacturers to work together on the same layout. Prior to this, command control systems were proprietary systems made by individual manufacturers, each using its own protocol. With DCC, decoders made by one company can be controlled by signals sent from another firm's DCC system.

DCC components

DCC systems consist of several components. Some systems are basic and can control only a handful of locomotives, while others have the potential to control hundreds.

An operator controls DCC-equipped locomotives with a cab (throttle). The cab can be integrated with other DCC components, tethered to the layout, or wireless. With a few exceptions, cabs are one of the components that can't be interchanged between different systems. Often a single manufacturer makes several styles of cabs for its DCC system, so you should be able to find one you like.

Just like a DC power pack, the cab has speed and direction controls. The speed control may be a knob, push button, or thumbwheel. The cab may have additional buttons to control "functions" as well. These are on-off switches that run accessories such as the locomotive's headlight, bell, and whistle.

The cab sends its instructions to the command station, which is the heart of the system. It converts the information from the cab to a DCC command that's sent through the rails. Before the DCC command can be used by a locomotive, its power must be increased by a booster. This device takes the raw DCC signal and increases the voltage to 12-20 volts.

In order to provide power for several trains at the same time, the booster must be capable of supplying several amps of current. Boosters typically supply from 3 to 10 amps or more. Multiple boosters can be used for large layouts that require more current.

The final piece of a basic DCC system is the locomotive decoder. There are decoders small enough to fit into Z scale locomotives and powerful enough to drive large-scale engines. Decoders are offered with various current capabilities for different motor sizes. For instance, a 1-amp decoder is typically needed for an HO locomotive.

Decoders

There are a number of ways to install a decoder into a locomotive. The easiest is with a drop-in ("plug-and-play") decoder. This type of decoder is designed for a specific locomotive, and it usually replaces the model's factory-installed light circuit board. These decoders require little or no soldering to install.

If there isn't a drop-in decoder available for your locomotive, you have two choices. Some locomotives have a socket for a plug-equipped decoder. There are also wired decoders that allow you to solder the wires directly to

The Model Rectifier Corp. Prodigy Advance control system includes a tethered cab, command station/booster, and 4-amp transformer.

The original lighting/circuit board on many locomotives can be replaced with a drop-in decoder in a few minutes.

the rail pickups, motor, and lights on the locomotive.

Decoders have a wide range of different features and options, including fine motor control, multiple lighting effects, and sound. Sound decoders are currently the fastest growing section of DCC, and many new locomotives are offered with factory-installed DCC sound decoders.

Sound decoders vary from basic to complex. Some decoders make generic sounds, while others generate prototype-specific effects. Companies now offer decoders that can be upgraded with downloadable sounds. An Internet connection and specialized hardware are required to download the sound files.

Other features

A DCC system can control other features of your layout beyond locomotives. Accessory decoders allow you to control signals, turnouts, drawbridges, and turntables, among other items.

DCC allows you to build your system as your knowledge and finances permit. You can get started for less than $200 and expand your system later, since many DCC systems are expandable.

DCC has been an exciting addition to model railroading, and it's likely to be around for many years to come. If you haven't given DCC a try, I hope you will. It not only enhances the sights and sounds of your models, it makes operations much more realistic.

DCC terms you should know

Power supply

Command station

Ammeter

Walkaround cab

Decoders

Track feeder wire

Wireless cab

Resistors

Those of you new to Digital Command Control (DCC), and even those who have a pretty good grasp on the basics, may benefit from a review of DCC terminology. I've divided the terminology into five categories.

Systems

Block: An electrically isolated section of track. This term is most often used in wiring DC layouts. On model railroads with DCC, it can be used for signaling or power districts.

Booster: A DCC booster is connected to the track. It "boosts" the DCC signal from a command station. Most systems accommodate multiple boosters to supply additional current needed for larger layouts.

Cab (or throttle): An operator uses a cab to control locomotives and wayside accessories. It's often a handheld walkaround style, but it can also be combined with other components and operated as a fixed cab.

Cab address: Some DCC systems require that cabs plugged into a bus have a unique identifier, called a cab address.

Cab bus: A cable run around the layout into which tethered cabs or other devices are plugged.

Command control: A method for controlling multiple trains on a single track. It can be analog, but is most often digital.

Command station: The brains of a DCC system. It takes commands from various cabs, converts them to DCC packets, and sends them to the booster.

Control bus: A separate cable that runs between the command station and all the boosters. Some systems combine the control bus with the cab bus.

Fixed cab: A cab integrated into another DCC system component, usually a command station.

Occupancy detection: Used to determine if locomotives or cars occupy a section of track.

Packet: A series of bits used to create a standard DCC command.

Power district: An electrically isolated section of track controlled by its own DCC booster. Sometimes sections isolated by DCC circuit breakers are referred to as power districts.

Track bus (or power bus): Two or more heavy-gauge wires carrying power from the boosters to the track. It can

also be used to power accessory decoders or layout lighting.

Wireless cab: A handheld cab that uses either radio or infrared light to communicate to the command station.

Decoders

Accessory (stationary) decoder: A specialized type of decoder that's generally used to control lineside accessories such as switch machines and lighting.

Address: Every decoder requires a unique identifier called an address. In the case of a mobile decoder, there are two different kinds of addresses—a short address (sometimes referred to as a two-digit address) and a long address (sometimes referred to as a four-digit address). Only one address can be active in a single decoder at a time.

Decoder: A small computer that responds to DCC packets. Mobile (locomotive) decoders control the motor, lighting, and sound effects.

Function buttons: Buttons on a DCC cab that are used to control the decoder's actions. They're generally referred to as F0, F1, F2, etc.

Function mapping: The method of assigning which button controls which function output or sound effect.

Function outputs: Wires on a decoder that power decoder lighting or other accessories.

Building locomotive consists

Consist: Two or more locomotives operated as one unit. The command station can be programmed to send individual packets to each locomotive from one cab command. Advanced consisting uses a decoder configuration variable (CV) temporally programmed to a consist address. In advanced consisting, the command station sends out one packet and all the locomotives programmed to that consist respond.

Speed matching: A method of customizing a locomotive's performance so that models from different manufacturers will operate smoothly together. This is accomplished through CVs.

Programming

Configuration variables (CVs): Memory locations in a DCC decoder that customize its performance. In some systems, DCC cabs program them. Configuration variables remain programmed even if power is removed. Some decoders can be programmed only on a programming track; others allow operations-mode programming.

Momentum: A way of simulating prototype train performance by slowing the locomotive's rate of speed change. It's controlled by CVs in the decoder.

Operations-mode programming: A method of programming CVs on the main line of a layout (also called programming on the main). Not all decoders or DCC systems support operations-mode programming.

Macro: A set of DCC commands that trigger a sequence of decoder functions or several decoders simultaneously.

Programming track: An isolated section of track connected to the programming terminals of a DCC system. It's used to program decoders.

Speed step: A setting on a DCC cab that controls the speed of a locomotive. There are 14, 28, or 128 speed steps in a DCC system. Most systems allow either 28 or 128 speed steps.

Speed table: A set of CVs used

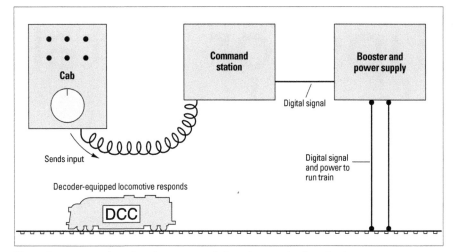

The cab, command station, booster, and decoder are the four basic parts to every Digital Command Control system.

to control the speed of a locomotive's motor at each speed step.

Electrical tools and terms

Alternating Current (AC): Electrical current that regularly reverses directions. The DCC signal to the track is considered AC; however, it isn't like household AC power and may be difficult to accurately measure with conventional meters.

Ammeter: A device that measures electrical current. It must be placed in series with the circuit. In DCC, it can be used to measure the current draw of a locomotive to help determine what decoder to install.

Ampere or amp (A): A unit of measurement for electrical current. A milliamp (mA) is $\frac{1}{1000}$ (.001) of an amp.

Automatic reversing (or auto reverser): A specialized DCC circuit that automatically reverses track polarity when it senses a short circuit. These are often used for wiring reversing loops, wyes, and turntables.

Bit: The smallest unit of digital data, with a value of 1 or 0.

Byte: A group of 8 bits.

Circuit: A path for electrical current. Most devices are connected to a circuit in parallel, series, or a combination of both.

Circuit breaker: A specialized circuit that shuts down power to a section of track if there is an electrical short.

Direct current (DC): A type of electrical current that flows only in one direction.

Power supply: A device that converts household AC into low-voltage DC to power a DCC system or accessory.

Pulse width modulation (PWM): How DCC decoders control a locomotive's motor speed. A series of full voltage pulses are sent to the motor. The longer in time the pulses are (the width), the faster the motor spins. Another form of PWM is used in a DCC packet to differentiate between a 1 bit and a 0 bit.

Rectifier: An electrical device made from one or more diodes that converts AC into DC.

Resistor: An electrical device that resists the flow of current. In DCC, it's commonly used when installing lighting in a locomotive. It either drops the voltage of a function output to match the requirements of light bulbs or limits the current of a function output when using light-emitting diodes.

Track feeders: Small-gauge wires between the track bus and the rails.

Transformer: A component that increases or decreases the voltage in an AC circuit. It can also be used to isolate one circuit from another. In DCC, transformers are generally used to power DCC systems that use an AC input.

Volt: A unit of electrical pressure. Household current in the U.S. is usually about 110V; an HO DC locomotive operates between 0 and 18V. The nominal voltage for a DCC system operating an HO layout is 14 volts.

Tips for installing decoders

By Cody Grivno

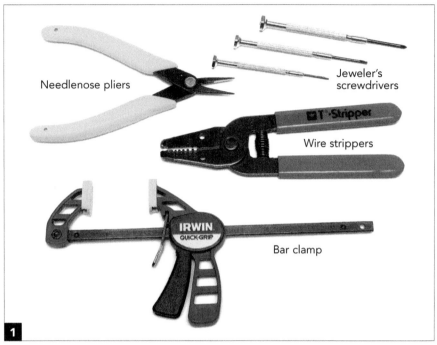

1

A variety of tools make decoder installation a snap, including needlenose pliers, screwdrivers, wire strippers, and a bar clamp. *Jim Forbes photos*

Ask a mechanic or construction worker what the key is to a successful job, and they'll tell you it's having the right tools. It's no different when installing DCC decoders. Without the proper tools, you can wind up with short circuits, sloppy solder joints, or—even worse—damaged decoders.

The tools shown here are some of the basics. You may have many of them at your workbench; others you may need to purchase. A good rule of thumb is to buy the highest quality tools you can afford. Yes, the up front expense may be a bit high, but when used correctly, these tools will last a lifetime. In the end, the right tools will make your decoder installations more professional and save you time.

Hand tools

Even a basic decoder installation requires hand tools. A set of jeweler's screwdrivers is a must for your workbench. Make sure the set includes straight slot and Phillips-head screwdrivers in various sizes. The screwdrivers are useful for removing screws that hold the body shell and draft gear boxes to the chassis and loosening the tabs that hold the shell in place.

In addition to screwdrivers, you'll want to invest in some specialty tools. A stripper designed for small-gauge wire will make it easier to remove insulation. Though most strippers include wire cutters, they're often too big for compact decoder installations. Instead, invest in a small pair of wire cutters that can get into tight spaces. Use the cutters only on copper wire, or you'll damage the cutting edges.

A couple of versatile tools are needlenose pliers and a bar clamp. The pliers are useful for forming and holding wire and small parts while solder-

ing. The clamp is handy for holding the halves of a split frame together while making cuts. All these hand tools are shown in **1**.

Electronic tools

There are electronic instruments, **2**, that help eliminate the guesswork from decoder installation. At the top of the list is a digital multimeter. This tool reads DC volts for measuring light bulb and decoder function voltage, DC amps for determining stall and bulb current, and ohms for measuring continuity and resistor values. The multimeter should be capable of measuring current up to 1 amp and 20 volts AC or DC.

To get the most bang for your buck, purchase a multimeter with an AC setting. This will help you determine DCC track voltage and make sure power districts are in phase on your model railroad.

Another read-out tool is the RRamp Meter from Tony's Train Exchange. This device determines the voltage and current of a DCC signal. It's also handy for determining the DC and DCC current draw before and after installing a decoder. The RRamp Meter also measures DCC voltage, making it a handy troubleshooting device.

Soldering

Although the wires on many of today's decoders are secured to circuit boards with plastic retainers, soldering is still the best way to achieve a reliable electrical connection. Photo **3** shows an Ungarmatic controlled soldering station. It features a heat-resistant holder for the iron and a sponge for cleaning the tip. Newer stations with the same features, as well as temperature control, are offered by Weller and Micro-Mark, among others.

In addition to a quality soldering iron, you'll need solder. Small-gauge (.025" to .032") flux-core solder works best for most decoder installations. Larger gauges of solder tend to flowinto circuit-board joints, causing short circuits and other problems. Acid-core solder isn't safe for electrical connections, as the acid, when combined with current flow, can lead to a cold or corroded joint over time.

Putty and tape

Poster putty, double-sided foam tape, and electrical tape, **4**, round out the tools list. If the decoder you install isn't secured with tabs or screws, poster putty or foam tape will do the trick. Some useful sizes of foam tape include ½" rolls, ½" x ½" squares, and 1" x 1" squares. You can find these items at most office supply stores or discount stores like Walmart, Target, or Kmart.

Electrical tape can be used to cover the bottom of a decoder (to prevent an electrical short) or insulate engine frames. It's also handy for covering soldered joints, although heat-shrink tubing is neater and more reliable over the long run.

Miscellaneous items

There are some convenience items you can add to your workbench as well. Most of today's locomotives are highly detailed. A foam locomotive cradle, such as the one from Bowser, **5**, will protect your engine as you work on it.

Decoder installation may require some math to calculate the value of

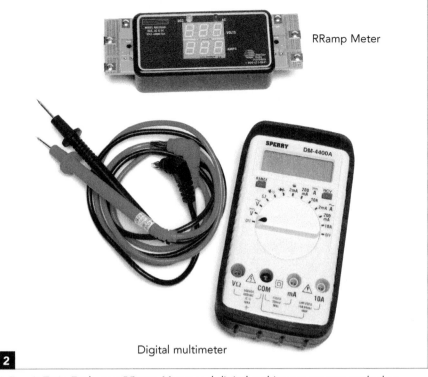

RRamp Meter

Digital multimeter

2

A Tony's Train Exchange RRamp Meter and digital multimeter are two tools that measure voltage and current.

configuration variables or dropping resistors. Having a calculator nearby makes it easier to figure these equations. Keep paper and a pencil handy to take notes.

If you'll be installing several decoders, have a supply of commonly used parts, including color-coded wire in various gauges, light-emitting diodes, light bulbs, and resistors.

To keep everything neat, I'd recommend getting a parts organizer (available in many styles and sizes at Lowe's, The Home Depot, and other home improvement centers) or supply drawers (available at discount stores).

Look for one with clear drawers, as it makes it easier to see what's inside. You can fill the unused compartments with other items, such as screws, couplers, and wheelsets.

It's best to build up your tool inventory over time. Start with the essentials, like jeweler's screwdrivers, wire strippers, a soldering iron, and solder. As you gain experience with DCC and tackle more complicated projects, you can add the specialized tools to your workbench.

If you're looking to make your next decoder installation easier and more enjoyable, give these tools a try.

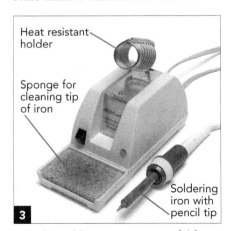

Heat resistant holder

Sponge for cleaning tip of iron

Soldering iron with pencil tip

3

A quality soldering station is useful for many hobby tasks. An iron with a pencil tip is ideal for decoder installation.

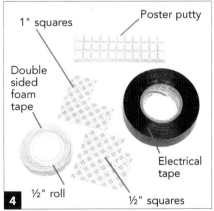

1" squares

Poster putty

Double sided foam tape

Electrical tape

½" roll

½" squares

4

Poster putty and foam tape are used to install decoders; electrical tape insulates engine frames and covers wire joints.

Foam locomotive cradle

Calculator

5

A foam locomotive cradle and a calculator are two convenience items to keep handy for decoder installations.

Solutions for short circuits

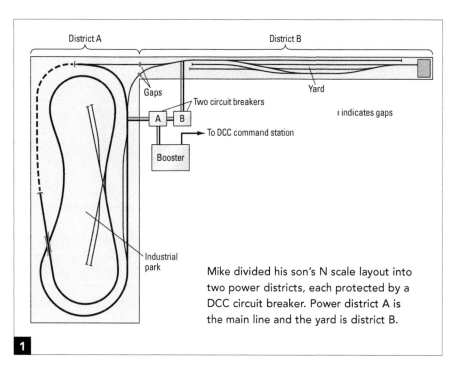

District A

District B

Gaps

Two circuit breakers

Yard

A   B

i indicates gaps

To DCC command station

Booster

Industrial park

Mike divided his son's N scale layout into two power districts, each protected by a DCC circuit breaker. Power district A is the main line and the yard is district B.

1

DCC power boosters have built-in, quick-acting circuit breakers. When a short circuit occurs, such as in a derailment or a locomotive running the wrong way into a turnout, the booster's circuit breaker shuts down power to the track. On a small layout with one operator, that's not much of a problem. However, on a large model railroad with many operators, this can be quite disruptive. To keep trains moving, you need to keep short circuits under control, and that is where power districts come in handy.

Power districts

A power district is any section of track that is electrically isolated from the rest of the railroad and is equipped with its own short-circuit protection. The layout shown in **1** has been divided into two power districts, each with its own circuit breaker. If a short occurs in the yard (district B), trains will still operate on the main line (district A).

There are several ways you can protect a power district when a short occurs. The best method is to equip each power district with its own DCC booster. However, that can be costly.

Another method uses automobile light bulbs, **2**. For DCC circuit protection, a single bulb (typically General Electric no. 1156) is placed in series with one rail in each power district. During normal operation, a very small amount of current flows through the bulb when a locomotive is running.

When a short circuit occurs, a much larger amount of current flows to the bulb, illuminating it. Once the bulb's filament is lit (heat increases its resistance), it protects that section of track from the short circuit. It also prevents the DCC booster's circuit breaker from tripping, allowing the trains in other power districts to keep operating. After the short is removed, the bulb dims and operation in that district can resume.

Still another option is to use DCC circuit breakers, **3**. In the example in **1**, one circuit breaker is wired between the DCC booster and each power district. When a short occurs, the circuit breaker trips before the booster's breaker does, isolating the problem to that power district.

All of these methods have pros and cons. Using separate DCC boosters for each district works well, but can be expensive. Automotive bulbs are a cheaper alternative, but only two or three HO locomotives can be run in such a power district. Digital Command Control circuit breakers are more expensive than bulbs but cost less than boosters.

I have two boosters on my HO scale Soo Line model railroad. Each booster powers a number of circuit breakers protecting different sections of the layout. This arrangement worked fine until I started using sound decoders. I noticed that when a locomotive with a sound decoder was in a power district protected by a circuit breaker during a short, the breaker didn't always reset.

To keep sounds from being interrupted by dirty track or intermittent connections, manufacturers equip their decoders with capacitors. Similar to a battery, capacitors store an electrical charge. When the track power is interrupted, the capacitor supplies the decoder with power for a short period. After the capacitor is discharged, it briefly draws a large amount of current. This is called in-rush current, which occurs when the power is restored and the capacitor is recharging.

Digital Command Control circuit breakers trip after detecting a short. After a few seconds, they reset automatically so operations can continue after the short is cleared. Some breakers read the in-rush from sound

To 1 rail

To DCC booster

General Electric no. 1156 bulb

2

Mike wires automobile bulbs in series with one of the rails. When a short occurs, the bulb's filament glows brightly. Heat increases the filament's resistance, isolating that section of track from the rest of the layout.

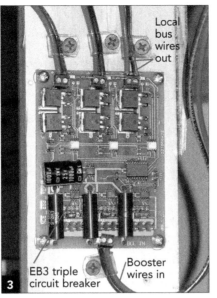

Local bus wires out

EB3 triple circuit breaker

Booster wires in

3

DCC circuit breakers work just like a breaker in your home. Mike split the output from his two boosters into nine power districts using NCE's EB3 triple breaker.

General Electric no. 1156 bulbs in parallel with NCE EB3 circuit breaker

4

Following NCE's directions, Mike wired these General Electric no. 1156 bulbs in parallel with the EB3 circuit breaker. When the breaker trips, current is diverted through the bulb.

decoder capacitors as a another short circuit and won't reset.

Although several companies offer circuit breakers, they don't all work alike. Some newer ones are designed specifically to distinguish between in-rush current and a short circuit. For example, the DCC Specialties' Power Shields on my layout work fine. However, I've had problems with other breakers.

Sound decoders aren't all the same either. The locomotives on my layout use Digitrax, ESU, QSI, and SoundTraxx products. I've found the most troublesome combination to be a QSI decoder (QSI is used by several locomotive manufacturers) and the NCE EB3 circuit breaker. This may vary from layout to layout depending on how the model railroad is wired and how many other loads (like passenger car lighting) are in any one power district. And, as DCC manufacturers improve their designs, this is becoming less of a problem.

Adjusting breakers

Some DCC circuit breakers have adjustments for the trip current and trip speed. I tried adjusting all of them on the EB3. Though no setting fixed

my problem, NCE has posted a work-around to the reset problem on the document archive section of its website: www.ncedcc.com/pdf/EB3%20 Sound%20Bypass.pdf.

The workaround, once again using an automotive light bulb, is shown in **4**. Under normal operation, the breaker provides a low-resistance path from the booster to the track.

When a short occurs, the breaker trips and the current is diverted through the bulb. The bulb then illuminates. After the short is cleared, the in-rush current flows through the light bulb, recharging the sound decoders, allowing the circuit breaker to reset normally.

The information from NCE says either a GE no. 1156 or GE no. 89 light bulb will work. I used the 1156 bulb, wired in parallel with the EB3 circuit breaker, as shown above. The breaker was able to reset with a dozen locomotives with sound decoders in the power district. Since I didn't have problems with my other circuit breakers, I didn't wire any bulbs with them.

Many DCC circuit breakers interrupt only one of the track wires. That's the terminal the bulb must be wired across. To determine which side of the

circuit is broken, use a voltmeter on the AC setting.

There are two terminals on the input side of the breaker and two terminals on the output side of the breaker. The meter must go between one input and one output terminal when power is applied. If you do this and have no AC voltage, try the other output terminal.

Next, induce a short circuit. If the voltage goes to zero, then that's the output terminal that's broken. Wire the bulb between that terminal and the opposite input terminal that you're measuring. If the voltage doesn't go to zero, move the voltmeter leads to the other input terminal and the other output terminal and try it again.

If you experience reset problems with your circuit breakers, the automotive light bulb may come to your rescue. It may take some experimenting with different bulbs, but it's likely you'll be able to solve the problem.

Though short circuits are frustrating, they don't have to bring your entire layout to a stop. With these techniques, you can contain a short to an isolated section of the railroad. This will keep the rest of your trains running and your operating crew happy.

2

Wiring tips

If you've wired a direct-current (DC) layout, you should be able to wire a model railroad for Digital Command Control (DCC). In fact, you can even convert an existing DC layout to DCC, as explained in a bit.

However, before doing so, take an inventory of your model railroad. For example, when determining the power draw, account for decoder-equipped locomotives, powered turnouts operated by accessory decoders, and illuminated structures, passenger cars,

and cabooses. It's also important to use the proper size wire for track buses and feeders, as explained on page 18.

In this chapter, we'll cover some suggestions for converting a DC layout to DCC, calculate the amount of power needed for a DCC system, add track buses and power districts, and use accessory decoders. We'll also look at how to make a yard control panel, wire reversing sections, and update an older DCC system.

10 tips for converting your layout to DCC

Many model railroaders start with layouts wired for direct-current (DC) operation. The spectrum runs from a single power pack with two wires to the tracks, to two-train operations with toggle-switch block control, to complex multi-train control with rotary switches, and reversing sections. In most cases, if your layout runs on DC, you can make it run on Digital Command Control. Here are 10 tips to help make the transition go smoothly.

1. Understand DCC system basics. A DCC system sends power and digital signals over the rails using alternating current (AC), which is present at all times. DCC systems have three basic components. The cab (or throttle) is what you control trains with, just like a DC power pack. It sends signals to a command station that takes information from all the cabs and converts it into combined digital signals. A booster takes those digital signals and amplifies them to provide enough power to run the trains.

Not all DCC systems have these components in separate boxes. Many

have all three (or the command station/booster) combined, but all the functions are still there.

2. Keep it safe. Wire your layout so that there are no shock or fire hazards, a concern because of the higher current of DCC. Most commercial DC power packs have their power supplies integrated. In other words, there's just one AC power cord from the cab to the wall outlet.

Many DCC systems require an external power supply or AC transformer. These can be purchased as a sealed unit with an integrated power cord from several DCC manufacturers, but some people opt to use a stand-alone transformer that must be wired. Either works fine, but a stand-alone transformer requires the power cord (primary side of the transformer) to be wired by the user. There should be a fuse wired on the primary side.

If you aren't comfortable wiring the 110-volt part of the circuit, hire an electrician (or just use a sealed unit). Under *no* circumstances should you wire a live circuit.

Make sure all 110V connections are covered to prevent an accidental short circuit. I've seen some transformers mounted under layouts with bare wires. *Don't do this.* Even if it's in a location where no one could come in contact with the high voltage, a dropped tool might. Short circuits can pose a fire hazard.

The secondary, or low-voltage, side of the transformer is less dangerous but still deserves respect. In a transformer, it's possible for the output to be a high potential to earth ground, presenting a shock hazard.

3. Know what you have. Many layouts are a patchwork of wiring, with odd bits of wire salvaged from other places, often in various colors, with little or no documentation of what the wires are for or where they go. Converting a layout wired like this to DCC can lead to all sorts of problems. There could be inadvertent connections (sneak paths) that could present a nightmare when trying to debug a DCC layout.

Before converting a DC layout to DCC, be sure you know what you have wired. Make sure there aren't multiple paths to feed any section of track from any DCC booster.

4. Plan the track bus. Adequate track wiring is a safety concern. DCC boosters supply more current than a DC power pack, and the track wiring on your layout must be capable of safely carrying this extra current.

A layout wired for DCC from the beginning usually has a track bus (two heavy wires) under the layout that supplies all the power for the locomotives on the layout. From that bus, smaller track feeders power each section of track. Small DC layouts may have just one or two pairs of track feeders from a single power pack to the railroad. To convert that layout to DCC, it might be a simple matter of replacing the DC power pack with a DCC system if the wiring is a sufficient gauge. On larger block control layouts, there may be a number of wires from a central control panel to each block. Again, as long as the wiring is a sufficient gauge, it should be fine.

The actual size of wire needed depends on the size of your DCC booster and the length of your run. The minimum recommendation is 16AWG. Your system manual will list the recommended wire gauges.

5. Have adequate block switches. If your layout is wired for block control and has a central panel with rotary or toggle switches that connect multiple throttles to the blocks, it might be possible to connect a booster in place of one of the throttles and set all the block switches to that throttle. If there are enough trains to require multiple boosters, a second booster can be substituted for another throttle. The layout can be divided into two sections by setting half of the blocks to one booster and half to the other.

A common problem with this type of conversion is that the block switch contacts (on toggle, rotary, or slide switches) might not be rated for the full current capacity of a booster. A short circuit on the track could damage the switch. Be sure to check the switch amperage ratings.

6. Make sure boosters are in phase. Even though the power DCC systems put to the track is technically AC, there's still a polarity. During one portion of the DCC cycle, one rail is a higher voltage than the other. During the next portion of the cycle, that rail is a lower voltage. The cycles change in millionths of a second. If two or more boosters are used, they must be kept in phase. At the block boundary where one booster is connected to the east side of the insulated joint and another booster is connected to the west side, it's possible to damage a locomotive that bridges the gap if the boosters aren't in phase. At the very least, a short circuit will occur, shutting down the DCC system.

To see if your boosters are in phase, use an AC voltmeter and measure across the same rail at the block boundary. The measurement should be less than a volt. If the measurement is 10-20 volts, the boosters aren't in phase. Correct this by reversing the wires on the output of one of the boosters.

If the measurement is more than a volt but less than 10 volts, something else could be wrong. The boosters may not be set at the same voltage, or there may be inadequate wiring. The boosters should be set at the same voltage. Check the system manual for instructions on how to adjust the voltage. Also, follow the manufacturer's instructions on grounding boosters. Multiple boosters require a common ground.

7. Don't use a common rail. I've never been a fan of common-rail wiring, even on DC layouts, but it's not recommended at all for DCC. This is especially true if you have multiple boosters, an auto reversing booster, or a DCC auto reversing module. If the boosters are ever out of phase, you risk doubling the voltage on locomotives and lamps and destroying them.

If you're converting a common-rail layout to DCC, cut block gaps in the common rail at the same locations as the other rail.

8. Don't mix DC and DCC. Though it might be tempting to keep a DC power pack connected to the layout, especially while converting a locomotive fleet from DC to DCC, I wouldn't recommend it. If a DCC booster and DC power pack accidentally connect by a locomotive running across the rail gaps between the two sections, you could damage one or both systems.

9. Have an adequate power supply. Some DCC systems require an external power supply. For larger systems, this usually means either an AC or DC power supply around 12-18 volts and 5-10 amps. It may be tempting to save money by powering your DCC system with your existing DC power pack, but it may not be the best idea. If the current rating isn't as high as the required current, it may appear if the DCC system is running correctly, but there could be problems.

The most obvious is that the DCC system won't be able to power as many trains as it normally could. Another concern is that the booster's circuit breaker may not be able to properly detect a short circuit.

10. Check your turnouts. You may have some trouble running trains over turnouts operating with DCC that worked fine with DC. It's likely that there are short circuits occurring as the locomotive runs through the turnout. While these shorts may go unnoticed with a DC throttle, the faster acting circuit breaker on a DCC booster may trip before the locomotive's flywheel can carry it through the turnout and clear the short. The auto reset on the DCC circuit breaker may take longer to clear the short. Eventually the circuit breaker will automatically reset, but not before the locomotive jerks or the sound system restarts.

Another problem I found on one of my old layouts that I converted to DCC was that the slide switches I used to carry power to each turnout frog were inadequate to carry the increased current a DCC system provides. Just a few times running up to the turnout lined the wrong way caused a short circuit and damaged the switch.

Calculating power for a DCC system

The number of locomotives on your model railroad is just one of many considerations when figuring power for a Digital Command Control system. *Bill Zuback*

The most common question I'm asked about Digital Command Control (DCC) is, "How much power do I need?" The question is usually followed by the layout owner telling me the size of his model railroad. Though size may give an indication, it doesn't directly affect the power required. The more important factor is how many locomotives will be run simultaneously.

Types of layouts
A small layout representing a portion of a busy industrial area or a passenger terminal with many lighted passenger cars might require more power than a large layout representing a branch line only running one train at a time.

Though modelers ask how much power they need, that's not the correct term. Power is voltage multiplied by the current (amps) and is measured in watts. Since the voltage of a DCC system is more or less constant, the better question is, "How much current do I need?"

A typical DCC system includes a booster that's either integrated into other system components or an additional box. It can supply anywhere from 1 to 10 amps. Except for the most basic, almost all DCC systems support extra boosters.

Each booster must be connected to a separate, isolated section of track. Unlike most DCC system components (except decoders), different brands of boosters can typically be mixed on a single layout and be driven by one

command station. Consult manufacturer manuals on how to do this.

Locomotives and decoders
Determining your layout's current draw isn't as simple as counting the number of locomotives on your model railroad and adding up the current, as shown in the illustration on page 17. If you just count locomotives, you'll be spending more on DCC components than you need. What matters is the number of locomotives running at one time.

Generally, the larger the scale, the more current the locomotive will draw. A locomotive with a heavy train going upgrade will draw more than that same locomotive running downgrade with just a caboose.

The age of the model is also another consideration. Older open-frame motors draw more current than newer can motors. For instance, an old Hobbytown HO locomotive will likely pull everything out of the yard, including the yard office. However, the original Pittman motor may draw an amp or more, while its modern equivalent may draw less than half that.

Sound decoders draw a lot of current, but mostly when first powered up. There are capacitors on the decoder that store energy so sound isn't interrupted over dirty track. On initial power up, the capacitors need to be charged, causing a large current draw for a short amount of time. This is called "in-rush" current.

I tested sound decoders from several manufacturers, and the most in-rush current I measured was about 150 milliamps (mA), but only for a couple seconds. After the capacitors charged, an idling locomotive with the sound on drew less than 10mA. One decoder, with all sounds on at factory default volume levels, drew 40mA.

Many decoder manufacturers produce motor-only decoders with capacitors designed to keep the motor running if track power is interrupted. These, too, have an in-rush current.

In-rush current is what causes some DCC circuit breakers to not reset after tripping when there are sound-decoder locomotives on the track. Except for the most extreme circumstances, almost all DCC boosters can handle in-rush current.

Lighting

Another source of current draw on a DCC system is lights on locomotives and in rolling stock like passenger cars and cabooses. The current draw of incandescent bulbs ranges from 20 to 50 mA. Light-emitting diodes are usually about 20 to 30mA. A passenger terminal might have dozens of stationary cars, but lighted, increasing the total current draw.

You might consider putting switches on your rolling stock to turn off lights that you don't need. Another option is to put in a lighting-only decoder (sometimes called a function decoder) to turn off rolling stock lighting from your DCC throttle when not needed.

Track-occupancy detectors and accessory decoders may also draw current from the DCC bus. Some of these devices are powered from external supplies, while others take all their power from the DCC connection. Being an electrical engineer, it seems like when I help people work on their layouts, I'm banished under the benchwork to do wiring. Perhaps this (and the fact that I'm 6'3") has caused my aversion to stringing wires under layouts. Therefore, I tend to use stationary decoders and track-occupancy detectors whose power comes from my DCC track bus rather than external power supplies.

If you use stationary decoders powered from the track bus on a layout with stall-type switch motors, the stall current will always be there when your DCC system is powered up. A Tortoise (Circuitron) machine draws around 15mA, a Cobalt machine draws around 30mA, and a Switch Master draws about 40mA. I have nearly 30 Tortoise machines on my layout, which adds about a half an amp to my DCC requirements.

Many modelers add another bus separate from the track bus to power turnouts and other accessories. They do this to keep power to the switch machines in the event of a short circuit (like a train running through an open turnout). This may be driven by a separate booster or an output of a DCC circuit breaker.

Power districts

Once the nominal current load has been added, you need to know where the current is being used. For this reason, layouts are normally divided into power districts. These are electrically isolated sections of track (on a DC layout they'd be called blocks) that allow for better distribution of power. If your current draw requires multiple boosters, you need to determine what sections of track each booster will power. For instance, a busy yard with numerous trains arriving and departing at the same time might need a dedicated booster (or two), while the rest of your

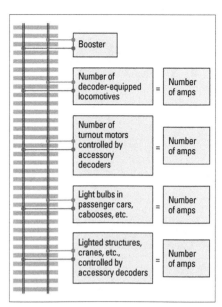

This illustration shows the various things to consider when determining the current draw on a model railroad.

layout might be powered from just one other booster.

Additional boosters may be necessary if your requirements don't split evenly with the booster capacity. That busy yard may require 6 amps, while rest of the layout may only require 3 amps. Though the total layout requirement is only 9 amps, 15 amps of "boost" is required—two 5 amp boosters in the yard and a single 5 amp booster for the rest of the layout. You might be tempted to try to carefully plan the exact requirements for each section, but that's often impossible to do. It's best to overestimate. I always round up a significant amount, as much as a third.

Wiring multiple boosters isn't hard, but you must follow the manufacturer's manual carefully. The booster power supplies must meet the specifications of the booster and must be wired correctly. Most manufacturers require a common connection between the boosters, but don't connect the outputs of the boosters together.

Figuring your power requirements isn't something you have to do right away. You may want to start with one booster and, as your layout requirements increase, add more. However, it's good to have a general idea of what your future requirements are so that you can wire your layout accordingly.

Track buses for DCC

A properly installed track bus—the heavy feeder wires that supply power to the track—is a key element of getting reliable operation from a DCC system.

Layouts wired for standard direct-current (DC) block control are divided into several isolated track sections called blocks. Each block has an electrical switch that controls which DC throttle powers that track section. In theory, a DCC layout could be wired as one large block with two wires feeding the power directly from the DCC booster to the track. However, on any model railroad larger than a test track, more wiring is necessary if you want your trains to run well.

Since DCC can power more than one locomotive at a time, more current is required to pass through the rails than with DC control. Small DCC systems usually have boosters that can supply at least 3 amps. Bigger systems can supply 5 amps, and large scale model railroads use boosters that can supply 10 amps. In DCC the voltage remains constant, and each locomo-

tive draws as much current as it needs at the time. A train going up a grade draws more current than a locomotive running by itself on level track. Locomotives in larger scales draw more current than those in smaller scales. The sum of all the current to each locomotive is what the DCC booster supplies. A medium-size HO layout with just a few trains with three locomotives each can approach the capacity of a single 5 amp booster.

Rail, wire resistance

So how do you get the current to the trains? Nickel silver rail is a poor conductor of electricity and acts like a resistor. The longer the rail, the more resistance there is. Following Ohm's Law, the more current going through a resistor, the larger the voltage drop from the booster to the locomotive.

I measured a piece of code 83

nickel silver rail and found the voltage drop was .057Ω per foot. That doesn't sound like much, but on anything but the smallest layout, it adds up quickly. At a full 5 amps, one piece of 3-foot flextrack fed at one end can cause a voltage drop of 1.7 volts at the other. How? Because the current must travel three feet down one rail, pass through the locomotive, and return three feet down the other rail. Imagine what it would be like on the other side of a large model railroad.

Feeding a layout with only two wires may not only affect locomotive performance, but it could be destructive. Since DCC boosters can supply more current than a typical DC throttle, they're equipped with internal circuit breakers that trip and remove power from the rails when a short circuit occurs. If not wired properly, the voltage drop through the rails may be

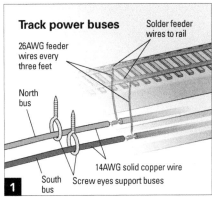

Track power buses

Solder feeder wires to rail

26AWG feeder wires every three feet

North bus

14AWG solid copper wire

South bus · Screw eyes support buses

1

For a track bus run of less than 30 feet, 14AWG solid copper wire is an ideal size. For runs longer than 30 feet, 12AWG solid copper wire is a better choice. Feeders should be added every three feet. Color code all wiring.

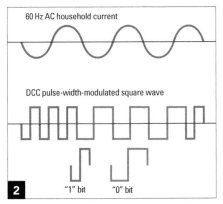

60 Hz AC household current

DCC pulse-width-modulated square wave

"1" bit   "0" bit

2

The AC power supplied to your house (top) has a curved waveform. Digital Command Control has a pulse-width-modulated plus or minus 14-volt square wave. The frequency of the DCC wave cycle is more than 140 times higher than household current.

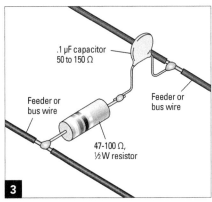

.1 μF capacitor 50 to 150 Ω

Feeder or bus wire

Feeder or bus wire

47-100 Ω, ½ W resistor

3

A capacitor and resistor in series can help dampen the distortion of DCC signals. NCE Corp. recommends a .1 microfarad (μF) capacitor and a ½-watt resistor around 50 to 150Ω. Digitrax doesn't recommend using a snubber on its system.

so great that the booster isn't able to detect a short. The full current capacity of the booster passing through whatever is causing the short circuit can be destructive enough to melt a brass truck frame.

Fortunately, copper wire has a much lower resistance than nickel silver rail. The solution to the voltage drop problem is to run a track bus of heavy-gauge copper wires beneath the layout, roughly parallel to the track, with smaller-gauge track feeders from the bus to the rails. The size of the wire required depends on the length of run and the capacity of your booster. There's no set maximum voltage drop that's acceptable, but it has to be low enough that the booster circuit breaker trips when a short occurs.

Each DCC manufacturer has different recommendations for acceptable wire size and length of wire runs. Different boosters may detect short circuits at different levels of voltage drop. It's important that the wiring is capable of handling the current output of the booster and that the booster circuit breaker will trip.

For boosters that supply 5 amps and less, 14-gauge (AWG) wire for runs of less than 30 feet is fine, **1**. If you have a longer run or larger booster, consider using 12AWG or heavier wire. You can determine the worst-case voltage drop by multiplying the wire resistance by your booster's full current capacity.

There is a handy calculator for this online at www.cirris.com/testing/resistance/wire.html. Enter the length of the run and bus wire size to determine the wire resistance. Remember to double the value to account for the voltage to the locomotive and the return.

There is debate about whether solid or stranded wire is better for track buses. Either will work. Digital Command Control is an AC waveform, so skin effect (AC flowing only through the outer layer of a conductor) will cause a slightly larger voltage drop in solid wire, but not enough to make a difference.

It's important to color code your bus wires to make sure that the same bus wire goes to the same rail throughout the layout. I use red for one rail and black for the other rail. From the track bus, smaller-gauge track feeders carry the current to the rail. I use 22AWG on my HO layout—smaller is fine for N scale. For short runs between the bus and the rail, the gauge of the track feeder isn't as important as the track bus gauge. Good electrical and mechanical contact to the rail is what's important.

Nickel silver rail is a poor conductor, but rail joiners are worse. Over time they will loosen and the rail will oxidize. It's a good idea to use feeders for every piece of rail and solder rail joints on short sections of rail.

Digital interference

DCC signals are square waves, **2**, and consequently generate a lot of noise at all sorts of frequencies. This can cause interference with a number of electronic devices, including your DCC throttles through the DCC cab bus. Though not a hard and fast rule, the track bus should be routed a foot or so away from the cab bus.

Another way to cut down on interference is to twist the bus wires a few times per every foot or so. Don't twist the bus so much that it is difficult to attach the feeders. Twisting the bus also has the effect of increasing the DCC signal fidelity. At the end of long buses, the square wave of the DCC signal can become distorted and cause excessive voltage that could potentially damage a decoder. NCE suggests placing a snubber, **3**, at the end of a long bus; Digitrax doesn't recommend using a snubber on its system.

As you wire your layout, frequently test your work by shorting the rails together at different locations. Your DCC booster should shut down. If it doesn't, check to make sure you have enough track feeders.

Dividing your track bus (and the track above it) into electrically isolated sections that are powered by additional boosters or protected by DCC circuit breakers will make it easier to diagnose short circuits.

Understanding power districts

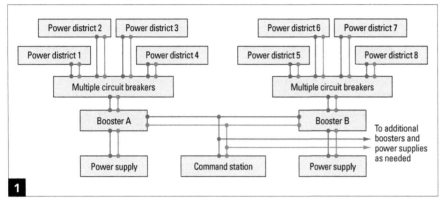

1

This diagram illustrates how to install multiple boosters. Since installation can vary between systems, follow the manufacturer's instructions carefully.

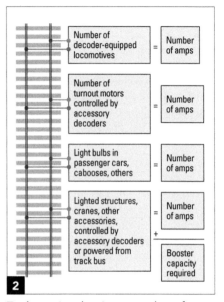

2

To determine the size or number of boosters you'll need, add up the current draw of your model railroad. This will give you the minimum requirement, but you'll probably want more should you decide to expand your layout.

Imagine you're operating a DCC layout with a group of friends. One of them is switching the paper mill, another is working the yard, and still another is running a hot passenger train. What happens when one of them runs through an open turnout or a locomotive derails? If the model railroad is wired as one block, all of the trains will stop and the dispatcher won't be thrilled when both passengers and freight are delayed while the problem is corrected.

For safety reasons, DCC boosters are equipped with circuit breakers that trip when a short circuit is detected. If only one booster powers your layout and a short occurs, the breaker will trip and there will be no power for the entire model railroad. Dividing your layout into separate electrical blocks, or power districts, isolates the short to a smaller area and allows trains in other districts to continue running.

Another benefit to dividing a model railroad into power districts is to increase the total power available to run trains. Further, it makes trouble-shooting short circuits easier.

Setting up districts

Power districts are usually set up as shown in **1**. A booster increases the power of the DCC signal created by the command station before it goes to the rails and also supplies power for locomotives and DCC-controlled accessories. On many simpler systems, the booster is integrated with the command station and perhaps a throttle or two. Boosters vary in the amount of current they can supply. Some small boosters have capacities of 2 or 3 amps, while the bigger ones can supply 8 or 10 amps. The size of booster you use is dependent on the amount of a load, or current draw, you have, **2**. Load is the total amount of current your entire layout will draw off the DCC booster.

Locomotives will probably be your biggest load. Typically the bigger the scale, the more current locomotives will draw. N scale locomotives usually draw around .25 amps (250 milliamps, or mA), HO locomotives can draw between 500 mA and 1 amp, S and O scale locomotives can draw up to 2 amps, and G scale locomotives can draw even more. Newer locomotives with can motors draw less current than older models with open-frame motors. Sound decoders further increase the power drain.

Passenger car lighting might be another big load if you have entire trains of cars powered from the track. A single light bulb can draw 10-100 mA. The sum current of all the bulbs is the total load.

Accessory decoders and the switch machines they control are another source of current draw. Stall-type switch machines draw approximately 25 mA all the time. On a large model railroad this could be significant.

Since DCC has a constant voltage

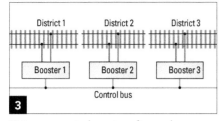

3

Using separate boosters for each power district prevents the entire layout from shutting down in the event of a short circuit. If a short does occur, only the trains in that district will be affected.

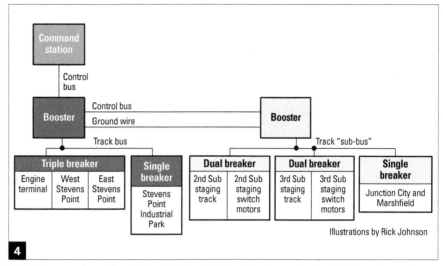

Illustrations by Rick Johnson

4

This diagram shows how Mike's HO scale Soo Line layout is wired. He used a variety of products to add more power and power districts.

on the rails, it's often a good source of low-voltage power for other things on your layout such as signals and structure lighting. If you have a lot of accessory lighting powered off the track, this needs to be taken into account as well.

Most larger DCC systems allow for the addition of extra boosters, but how each one is wired varies between manufacturers. This is also an exception to the rule that, other than decoders, components of different DCC systems aren't compatible with each other. Some boosters can be used with other DCC manufacturer's command stations, but the wiring instructions in the system manuals must be followed closely. Pay special attention to grounding and using external power supplies. This applies when using boosters from the same manufacturer as your DCC system.

To wire the output of the boosters to the track, you first must make sure the track sections they're being attached to are electrically isolated and the track buses are separated, **3**. If your layout loops back on itself in a continuous loop, make sure both ends of the power district are isolated.

Next, connect each booster to its isolated section of track. Then check the "phase" of each booster. Digital Command Control is AC, which means that current flows in both directions, but at different times. At a given time (measured in microseconds), the right rail will be a higher voltage than the left. A few microseconds later, the right rail will be a lower voltage than

the left.

To be in phase, the right rail of the track supplied by one booster must be higher than the left at the same time as it is on the track supplied by the other booster. If it isn't, the locomotive may stop when crossing power districts. Even worse, it may damage your locomotive.

To check the booster phase, use a multimeter set on the AC volts setting and measure across the gap between power districts on the same rail. The reading should be near zero. To double check the phase, measure the voltage from the north rail on one side of the gap to the south rail on the other side of the gap. It should be around track voltage, which on most DCC systems is 14 volts. If the phase is incorrect, simply reverse the connections at your booster.

DCC circuit breakers

Another way to divide your layout into power districts is to use DCC circuit breakers. Installing breakers doesn't increase the power to your layout, but they're a convenient way to add power districts and are very reliable.

Again, the track and associated bus must be divided into separate sections. Then add the circuit breaker between the booster and the track bus. Most

of the time, both rails go through the circuit breaker. Just like adding extra boosters, the phase must be checked when installing circuit breakers.

If your turnouts are controlled by accessory decoders, you should consider adding a circuit breaker exclusively for them. Should a locomotive run through an open switch, a short circuit is likely to occur, tripping the track breaker. If the same breaker controls both the track and switch machines, there will be no power to properly throw the turnout.

Even electrical switches isolating sections of track will aid in finding a short, though it's not automatic and won't keep other trains from stopping. If you converted your layout from DC block control to DCC, the block switches can be shut off one at a time to help locate the problem.

I use a combination of boosters and circuit breakers to power my model railroad, **4**. I have two boosters, each controlling about half the layout. The section powered by each booster is further divided by circuit breakers into power districts.

Almost any layout being operated by more than one person can benefit by adding power districts. Just remember that if you have a large load, adding multiple boosters is a requirement.

Accessory decoders for your layout

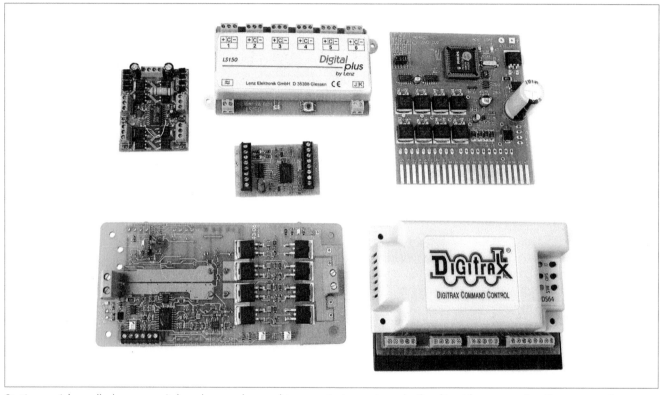

Stationary (also called accessory) decoders can be used to operate turnouts and other lineside accessories. Some examples (clockwise from lower right) include the Digitrax DS64, DCC Specialties PSX-ARFB, NCE Switch It, MRC 1628, Lenz LS150, and CVP Products AD4HC.

Most users of DCC are familiar with mobile, or locomotive, decoders. Each locomotive on a DCC layout needs one to operate. But there's another type that you might not be as familiar with: the accessory, or stationary, decoder.

As the name implies, accessory decoders are intended to control turnouts and other lineside accessories. Several companies manufacture accessory decoders, including firms that don't make DCC systems or mobile decoders. Thanks to the National Model Railroad Association's (NMRA's) DCC standards, the decoders will work with systems made by other companies. However, some basic DCC systems can't issue the necessary commands to operate accessory decoders.

Types of switch machines

There are three types of switch machines, and there are accessory decoders designed to operate each one. Slow-motion motors, such as Tortoise, Cobalt, and Switch Master, require constant power. They're actually a DC motor that stalls when the points of the turnout have reached the stock rail. Power is on at all times. Bipolar switch machines (Kato and LGB) and twin-coil machines (Atlas and NJ International) require a large surge of current to snap them into place.

Bipolar machines have a single coil, and the direction of electrical current determines the direction the points a realigned.

Twin-coil machines have two coils.

If power is applied to one coil, the turnout lines in one direction. If power is applied to the other coil, the turnout is thrown in the opposite direction.

Because of the power requirements for each switch machine, different accessory decoders, or at least unique configurations for a single type of accessory decoder, are needed to control them.

Accessory decoders let you use a throttle to line turnouts, but they have other advantages as well. Though it varies between brands, the decoders are often simple to wire. Only four wires are required (two for the track bus and two for the switch machine) for the simplest decoders. As with mobile decoders, accessory decoders get power and commands through the track bus.

The NCE Switch It can power two turnout motors. Mike attached the accessory decoder to a Tortoise switch motor with double-sided foam tape.

Some decoders, however, require a separate power source. On some brands either external push buttons or DCC commands may be used to actuate the decoder.

There are also feature-rich accessory decoders. Some can be programmed to set up routes and a host of other things. An example of a route is a yard throat where several turnouts need to be lined for a train to arrive on a particular track. If your DCC system is so equipped, routes can also be set up as macros. A macro is a series of accessory decoder commands programmed into a DCC system so that when it is selected by a throttle, all of the commands are executed.

Some decoders can be programmed to detect an approaching locomotive and automatically align the turnout. Others can provide feedback of a turnout's position directly to a computer for use by a Centralized Traffic Control (CTC) board or signal system.

Programming

Accessory decoders require a unique address in order for the DCC system to send commands to them. Unlike a mobile decoder, however, it's not convenient to put them on a programming track, especially after they're wired and installed. They often have a jumper that allows the decoder to be programmed using the track bus rather than the programming track, similar to operation-mode programming on a mobile decoder.

The more features an accessory decoder has, the more programming is required. This doesn't mean the programming has to be complicated. Like other aspects of DCC, it's best to use the basic functions first and attempt more difficult tasks as you become more comfortable with the decoder.

Although accessory decoders are primarily used with turnouts, they have other applications. For example, I used a CVP AD4MC accessory decoder to control a bascule bridge on a friend's layout. Because of the NMRA standards, any DCC system that can issue accessory decoder commands is able to control it, not just CVP's Easy DCC system.

An accessory decoder can control other layout animation effects, such as crossing gates and semaphore signals. The key is matching the electrical requirements of the animation equipment to what a decoder can supply. In the case of the bascule bridge, it required about 200mA at 6 volts (V) for at least a minute. The AD4MC is designed to work with bipolar machines and is programmed to pulse 250mA at 12V for about 200 milliseconds.

That doesn't sound like a match, but the AD4MC can be programmed to be on continuously. The bridge has a limit switch that shuts off power when it reaches the end of its travel. The decoder is able to supply more than the 200mA required for the motor, so I lowered the voltage by connecting four bridge rectifiers in series with the bridge motor.

Accessory decoders can add a new dimension to your DCC system. There's such a wide variety available that you should be able to find something that fits your needs.

Simple yard control panels with DCC

Turnouts and other accessories can be controlled with a Digital Command Control throttle and push buttons. This panel controls turnouts at a staging yard on Mike's HO scale Soo Line layout.

DCC systems allow you to do a lot with the hand-held throttle. Most let you control turnouts with special commands and accessory decoders. Sometimes, though, it's still desirable to control accessories with a push button in the fascia. NCE's Mini-Panel, among other products, allows you to do just that.

Designing a panel

I have a 10-track staging yard representing the territory both east and west of the modeled section of my HO scale Soo Line layout and another representing the Nekoosa line south of Marshfield, Wis. Both the west end and Nekoosa line staging yards are behind backdrops and require remote-controlled turnouts.

I wired a DCC accessory decoder to each turnout motor in the yard so I can align the switch points with a throttle. I also have macros set up in my DCC system that allow me to issue programmed multiple-accessory commands with one throttle command. This lets me set up routes and align the necessary turnouts. I set up the commands so the track number corresponds to the macro number.

When I host operating sessions, I use two-man crews. Not only is this more prototypical, but it's a good way to break in new crew members. I want the engineer (who's holding the throttle) to concentrate on running trains and the conductor to line the turnouts. To support this, I designed a control panel with a track diagram and push buttons at turnout locations.

Back in the days of twin-coil switch machines, I used diode routing to line multiple turnouts to a desired track. Though a similar but more complicated circuit can be used with slow-motion switch motors, mine were already wired to accessory decoders.

Several accessory decoders have external inputs that let you push a button to activate the decoder through the DCC system. However, this doesn't allow for route control.

Fortunately, there are specialized components that allow programmed route control using DCC. NCE's Mini-Panel is basically the firm's throttle with switch inputs instead of a key-

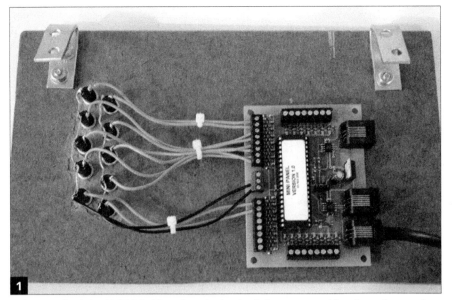

When the Pro Cab is connected to the Mini-Panel's programming jack, it works as a programmer instead of a throttle. The display screen leads you through the programming process.

Mike attached the NCE Mini-Panel to the back of the tempered hardboard control panel with double-sided foam tape. One wire from each push button is connected to the Mini-Panel.

pad interface. It has 30 inputs that can be connected to push buttons, block detectors, toggle switches, and micro-switches, among other items. The user programs the Mini-Panel to execute a series of up to four commands when a particular input is grounded. These can be accessory commands, macros, signal commands, or locomotive commands. If more than four commands are needed, multiple inputs can be linked together or macros can be used.

Though NCE's Mini-Panel is flexible, it can't be used with other DCC systems. If you have a Digitrax system, Team Digital's (www.team-digital1.com) SRC16 is somewhat similar. The SRC16 also has modes that operate with other DCC systems, but it won't originate DCC commands in that way. See the April 2008 DCC Corner in *Model Railroader* for more on accessory decoders.

Since I have an NCE system, I use NCE's Mini-Panel to control the staging yards on my layout. It was easy to program and the wiring couldn't have been simpler.

I drew a track diagram of the ladder of my staging yard using Atlas' Right Track freeware track planning software. Atlas no longer offers the software for download, but any model railroad CAD program will work just fine (as will most other drawing programs). I

printed the diagram on colored paper and laminated it to a piece of tempered hardboard as the photo on page 24 shows.

I then mounted 10 push buttons, one for each track, on the board and mounted the Mini-Panel to the back side of the panel with double-sided foam tape, **1**. I connected one wire from each button to an input on the Mini-Panel. I wired the other side of the buttons to the Mini-Panel's ground. The only connection to the rest of the layout is via the DCC cab bus. The control and power for the Mini-Panel comes through the cab bus just as if it were a throttle.

The Mini-Panel has three RJ-12 jacks. Two are for the cab bus—one jack is the bus in, and the other is the bus out. The other RJ-12 plugs into a Pro-Cab throttle and is used for programming.

Programming

Programming the Mini-Panel was easy and clearly explained in the instruction manual. When the Pro-Cab is plugged into panel's programming jack, it functions as a programmer instead of a throttle.

The display guides you through the programming process, **2**. It asks which input you want to program (INP: 01 on the screen) and what commands

you want to execute. Since I already had my routes programmed as macros (macro number: 029 as shown above), it was a simple matter of programming which macro was to be associated with which input.

Block detectors may also be used as inputs, making it possible to have a command associated with a loco-motive's location on the layout. For example, a turnout can be automated to line itself for an approaching train or a track derail can be set to protect an open lift-out section so a train doesn't run off the edge of the layout.

The Mini-Panel can also control locomotives. Combined with block detectors and accessory decoders, rudimentary train automation can be achieved. This could be used for a dis-play layout or other applications.

The Mini-Panel includes "delay" and "wait" commands to further aid control. The "skip" command allows users to combine inputs to execute different commands based on the com-bination of multiple inputs.

My dispatcher's desk is next to one of my staging yards. The Mini-Panel for that staging yard has available inputs, which I eventually used for dispatcher-operated train-order signals (see page 86).

Controlling turnouts and other accessories is one of the many features of a DCC throttle. However, products like NCE's Mini-Panel (among others) make it easy to also control accessories with push buttons.

Block detection and DCC

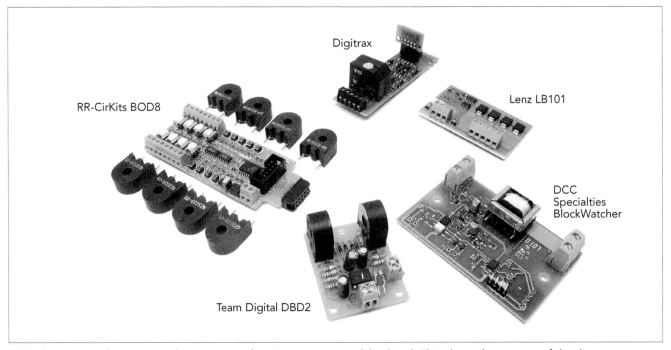

Block detectors make it easy to determine train locations on your model railroad. This photo shows some of the detectors available that are compatible with Digital Command Control.

As your layout grows, you may find it necessary to determine if a section of track is occupied by a train. This could be a block for a signal system, a section of hidden track, or a helix.

There are several ways to determine if a track is occupied. A photo sensor between the rails and an overhead light source is a popular optical method. If you're simply trying to determine the occupancy of hidden tracks, you could use a mirror or video camera.

Another common way to detect occupancy is by sensing electrical current passing through the rails and rolling stock. For this technique to work reliably, each piece of rolling stock must draw current. Locomotives, lighted passenger cars, and lighted cabooses work well, but other rolling stock must have resistive wheelsets. These are available commercially or can be made using surface-mount-device (SMD) resistors, **1**.

Signaling

A variety of signal systems are available today. Most offer a block detector that's compatible with DCC. There are also a number of DCC block detectors made by firms that don't offer signal systems.

Until control systems like DCC were introduced, model railroads were often controlled with direct-current (DC) cabs. Some current-sensing detectors designed for DC may not be compatible with DCC, so it's a good idea to test them first.

Most current-sensing block detectors can be divided into two types. The first may be put in series with one of the rails. The current passes through a resistor or diode, causing a small voltage across it that is measured and used to determine if there's current above a designated amount. Circuitry on the block detector detects the voltage and reports if the block is occupied.

The second type uses a coil that the block feeder is fed through. It takes advantage of DCC being alternating current (AC) and acts like a transformer to create a detectable voltage.

Some detectors also have a way to adjust how much current is needed to indicate a positive detection. The method varies between detectors. In all types of current detection, the current going to the block must pass through the detector. There can't be any sneak paths for current to go directly to the rail without going through the detector.

To wire a layout for DCC, it's best to have a track bus consisting of two heavy-gauge wires below the benchwork under the track. The DCC booster feeds the bus, and track feeders are run between the bus and the rails to power the track.

When adding block detection in addition to the main bus, a sub bus

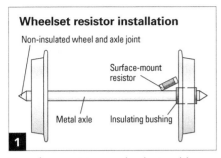

Wheelset resistor installation

Non-insulated wheel and axle joint

Surface-mount resistor

Metal axle

Insulating bushing

1

To make a resistance wheelset, solder a surface-mount resistor across the insulated bushing on a metal wheelset.

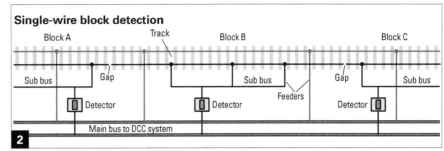

Single-wire block detection

Block A · Track · Block B · Block C

Sub bus · Gap · Sub bus · Gap · Sub bus

Detector · Feeders · Detector · Detector

Main bus to DCC system

2

When adding block detection, track feeders for each block should be attached to the sub-bus rather than the main bus. The wire attaching the sub bus to the main bus passes through the detection circuit.

must be created, **2**. The track feeders for the block are attached to the sub bus rather than the main bus. Also, gaps must be cut in the rail at either end of the block. All connections between the main bus and the sub bus are made through the block detector.

Depending on the block detector, the sub bus can either be a single wire or one for each rail. Some block detectors require that power from both bus wires be fed through it; others require only one. For detectors that require one, the sub bus only has to be one wire, and only one rail has to be gapped.

Some detectors are capable of detecting multiple blocks. This is cost effective if several blocks are close to one another, such as an interlocking plant. However, block detectors usually have to be located near the block they are detecting. Since DCC is AC, any stray capacitance causes a leakage current. That current may give a false occupancy indication.

Some detectors require external power supplies, while others receive their power directly from the DCC system. How the block detector relays occupancy information also varies between brands. Some detectors are designed to work with a specific signal system, and some interface only with components from the same company. They can report back occupancy to either a stand-alone signal system or a computer. Other detectors are generic and can interface with a variety of other circuits.

I designed my own automatic block signals using a Programmable Logic Device (PLD). For the system to work, I needed a block detector. I used the

NCE BD20, which works well with my system. The BD20, **3**, requires the block current to pass through its coil. My track bus is made of black and red wires. Track feeders for the north rail are attached to the red wire, and feeders for the south rail are attached to a sub bus for that specific block. Connection between the sub bus and the black wire of the main bus is made through the coil of the BD20.

I used two 10KΩ resistive wheelsets from Logic Rail for each piece of rolling stock. I used two because dirty rails can prevent constant wheel-to-rail contact, making it possible for the rolling stock to escape detection with just one wheelset.

My DCC system is set to 14 volts. Using Ohm's Law, I calculated that a single 10K wheelset would draw about 1.4mA (14V/10,000Ω). The sensitivity of the BD20 is adjusted by the number of turns through its coil. By examining the charts on the back of the BD20, I found that I would need about five turns to detect a single wheelset. Unfortunately, with my 5-amp DCC booster, only four turns are allowed on the BD20. As it turned out, my signal system had less of a load on the detector output than I thought. Three turns through the coil was enough to detect a single wheel set.

The output of the BD20 is an open-collector transistor, which means there are two terminals. The first, the emitter, is tied to the ground of the signal system. The second, the collector, is tied to a logic input in the signal system. Most signal systems have inputs that are tied to some voltage through a resistor. This is required for the open-collector output found on the BD20.

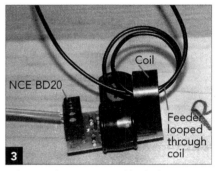

Coil

NCE BD20

Feeder looped through coil

3

Mike used NCE's BD20 block detector on his HO scale Soo Line layout. Connection between the sub-bus and the black wire of the main bus is made through the BD20's coil.

My system is tied to 3.3V with a weak (high-resistance) pull-up resistor that's built into the PLD. With no current in the block, the transistor is off and the collector is at 3.3V. That's considered a "1" to the PLD.

When current flows into the block, the transistor is turned on and the collector connects to the emitter, making the collector ground, or "0." The PLD detects that its input went from 1 to 0 and knows the block is occupied.

If you're using a signal system that requires a computer for logic, an interface is required between the detector and the computer. Digitrax, Lenz, and NCE, among others, offer modules that interface block detectors to their respective cab buses. They also make other modules that connect their cab buses to computers. JMRI, KAM Industries, and Railroad & Co. offer computer programs to control signals.

The use of block detectors can add a new dimension to your layout. There are numerous choices that work well with DCC. Shop around and see which one works best for you.

Wiring reversing sections for DCC

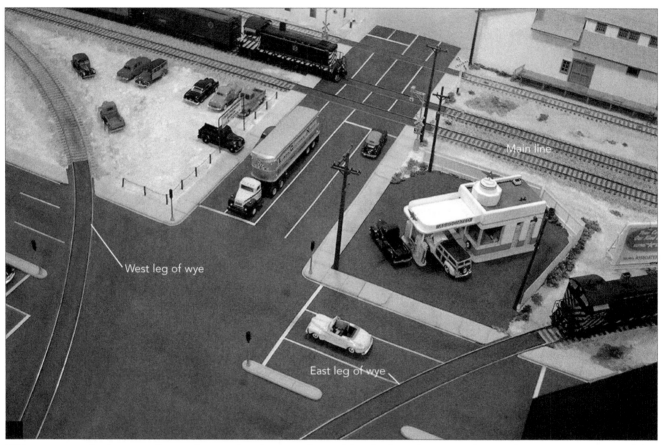

West leg of wye

East leg of wye

Main line

Wiring a wye and other reversing sections, such as loops and turntables, for Digital Command Control requires special attention to avoid short circuits. *Keith Jordan*

Reversing sections such as wyes, loops (balloon tracks), and some turntables require special attention when wiring your layout for DCC. Even though DCC is technically AC, it still has a polarity like direct current (DC). At any instant, one rail has a higher voltage than the other. Tens of microseconds later they switch, and then the first rail has a lower voltage then the second.

This causes a problem when a reversing section is used. Some track arrangements that create a reversing section aren't obvious. If the wheels on the engineer's side of a locomotive are in contact with one rail and, without

lifting the locomotive from the tracks, the locomotive can move such that the wheels on the engineer's side now contact the other rail, there is a reversing section. Without gaps in the rail, this causes a dead short between the rails as shown in **1**.

Any method that can be used to control a reversing section on a DC layout can also be used with DCC, provided the electrical switch contacts are capable of handling the extra current capacity of a DCC booster. If track power is interrupted, such as when flipping a toggle switch to reverse track polarity, DCC sound decoders may restart.

The classic way to wire a reversing section on a DC layout is to isolate a section of track within a loop or on one leg of a wye and feed the track power to that section through a double-pole, double-throw (DPDT) switch, **2**. With this, a train enters the isolated section of track and stops. Once the turnout is aligned and the engine and switch are reversed, the train can continue through the rest of the reversing section.

This technique will work with DCC as well. However, since track polarity has nothing to do with the direction of a train in DCC, stopping the train and reversing direction with the throttle isn't necessary.

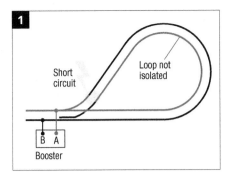

There is the potential for a short circuit any time a track turns back upon itself. To correct this problem, you must be able to change the reversing track section's polarity.

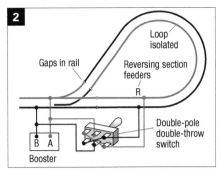

In this arrangement, an isolated section of track is connected to a power source through a DPDT switch. This is probably the simplest way to make reversing section.

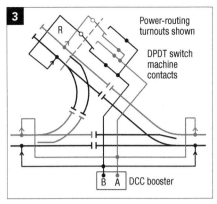

If a single leg of a wye is longer than the longest train on the layout, it can be used as a reversing section. Just isolate the section of track and wire it with a DPDT switch as shown above.

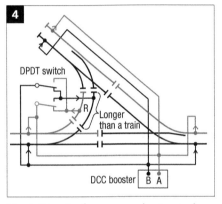

The tail track of a wye can be treated in the same way as a manual reverse loop, as long as it doesn't connect with another section of the model railroad.

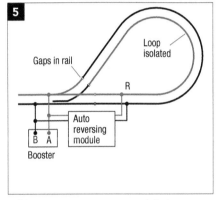

Adding an auto-reverse module is as easy as connecting it between the booster and isolated loop. These modules are available from several makers.

Auxiliary turnout contacts can often be used to control reversing sections. On a loop, the balloon track must be completely isolated from the turnout leading into it. The polarity is then controlled by the DPDT contacts in the turnout.

The tail of a wye track can be treated in exactly the same way, as long as it doesn't connect with any other section of the layout, **3**. Alternately, a single leg of a wye that's longer than the longest train can be isolated and wired with a DPDT switch, **4**.

Many of today's commercial turntables have a split pit rail or a commutator that accomplishes polarity reversal automatically, but these may result in momentary shorts or current drops that cause headlights to switch on and off and sound decoders to restart. My Stevens Point roundhouse turntable was scratchbuilt and doesn't have a built-in reverser. Though I could have added a DPDT switch to the track feeders, I used a DCC auto reverser instead.

Auto-reversing modules

Digital Command Control technology allows for another method of controlling reversing sections. Digitrax, Lenz, Model Rectifier Corp., and Tony's Train Exchange (among others) sell auto-reverse modules that replace the traditional DPDT switch, **5**.

In addition, Tam Valley Depot recently released an automatic reversing circuit that can be adapted for reversing sections. You can read a review of its Hex Frog Juicer in the February 2010 *Model Railroader*.

Auto-reverse modules rely on a short circuit occurring and being detected. When the module detects a short, it reverses the polarity of the isolated section so quickly that the booster doesn't shut down.

There are two basic types of auto-reverse modules: solid-state and relay controlled. The solid-state modules are a bit faster and will never wear out, but they're usually more expensive. Speed is an issue because the module must detect and reverse polarity before the circuit breaker on the booster (or an external circuit breaker) trips. Also, the faster the auto reversing module can change the polarity, the less likely it is that your sound decoders will restart.

In addition, the module must reverse at a lower current than a circuit breaker will trip. Some auto-reverse modules allow adjusting the param-

eters with a potentiometer, jumpers, or configuration variables (CVs). But even with the adjustments, not all modules are compatible with all power-supply circuit breakers.

It's usually safe to use an auto-reverse module from the same manufacturer as your booster or external circuit breaker. When in doubt, read the instruction manual or visit the manufacturer's website. There are also some DCC discussion groups online with members who are willing to help. Odds are good that someone has tried the combination you're considering.

Wiring a reversing section on a DCC layout is no harder than on a DC model railroad. However, with the aid of DCC auto-reverse modules, operating through a reversing section is much easier.

Update an older DCC system

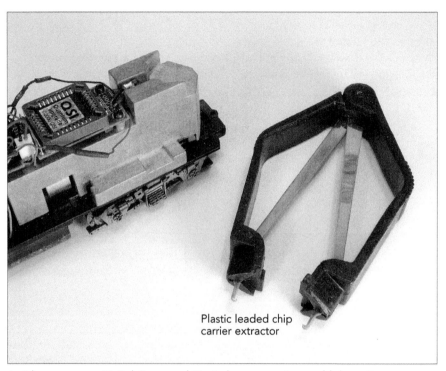

Plastic leaded chip carrier extractor

Just because your Digital Command Control components are old doesn't mean they're obsolete. Mike explains how to replace plastic leaded chip carriers and perform other upgrades.

When you purchased your Digital Command Control (DCC) system, you no doubt did your homework and bought the system that was best for you at that time. However, your needs may have changed and DCC, like most technology, is moving forward. Can your DCC system keep up?

If your requirements change and you need to run more trains with more operators, simply adding more throttles and/or more boosters may be enough. Most larger systems allow for expansion. Smaller starter systems like the Digitrax Zephyr and NCE PowerCab are specifically designed for expansion by adding boosters and throttles. The Zephyr and Zephyr Xtra also support a larger command station while allowing you to use the original Zephyr as a throttle.

Similarly, the NCE PowerCab allows the addition of the SB3a Smart Booster to increase capability. If you purchase NCE's feature-rich Powerhouse Pro, you can still use the PowerCab throttle.

Even if you have a large DCC system, your throttles may no longer serve your needs. For example, some sound decoders now support 28 functions. Just a few years ago, DCC throttles didn't support that many functions. With upgrades, you can take advantage of these new functions without buying new equipment.

Many companies have also updated their throttles over the years. Model Rectifier Corp., CVP, Digitrax, and NCE, among others, have introduced upgraded throttles since their systems debuted. Their systems allow you to mix and match old and new throttles on the same system. Of course, the manufacturer of your new throttle must be the same as the manufacturer as your DCC system. You can't mix and match.

Many systems also allow you to upgrade the features of your DCC system, throttles, or decoders by updating their firmware. Not only can new features be added, but bugs with the original firmware can be fixed. Even better, you don't need to buy new components.

Hardware, software, firmware

Most of us are familiar with hardware (an actual electronic component) and software (a computer program that can readily be changed). Halfway in between is firmware. Firmware is similar to a computer program, but it's loaded into the microcomputer memory in a DCC component from an integrated circuit (IC chip) called a PROM (Programmable Read Only Memory). The contents of a PROM remain even when power is removed. By reprogramming the firmware in the PROM, the behavior of the microcomputer can be changed.

For many years systems like CVP's Easy DCC and NCE's Powerhouse Pro have featured firmware updates by issuing new PROMs. Replacing PROMs requires some skill, but anyone can do it with a little patience and minimal tools.

Static electricity can damage integrated circuits, so you need to take some precautions. You can reduce static electricity by using a static mat, keeping the air from getting too dry, and touching ground prior to handling IC chips. Static mats and wrist straps are available at RadioShack and electronics distributors.

Programmable Read Only Memory

comes in different packages or shapes. The two most common in DCC systems are the DIP (Dual In-line Package) and the PLCC (Plastic Leaded Chip Carrier). The DIPs, shown at right, are rectangular with pins along the two long sides.

The DIPs can usually be removed with a small screwdriver. Work slowly so you don't bend the pins. The DIPs also must be put in the same way they came out. One corner of the chip has a mark indicating that it's pin 1. Pin 1 of the new chip must be oriented in the same corner of the socket as the old chip. Often a "1" is silk screened on the printed-circuit board to avoid confusion.

The PLCCs are square chips with the leads curled underneath them. Removing the old PLCC PROMs is best done with a special extractor like the one shown at left. It's available from RadioShack (item no. 276-2101) and other electronics distributors.

Replacing a PLCC PROM is fairly easy. One corner of the chip is cut at a 45-degree angle, and the socket has a corresponding portion filled in so the chip can only be oriented one way. Applying even pressure to all sides when inserting the chip will ensure a smooth installation.

Several companies like Digitrax, Lenz, MRC, and NCE offer throttle upgrades by sending the component back to the factory for updates. Digitrax offers Update an older Digital Command Control system upgrades of its UT4 throttle to the UT4R (radio) or UT4D (duplex radio). Likewise, you can update Digitrax's DT400 throttle to a DT402 throttle (tethered, radio or duplex radio). Once the DT400 throttle is updated to a DT402, you can add future firmware updates. You must download a PROM file from the manufacturer's website and connect your cab bus LocoNet to a computer using a computer interface.

Lenz has a similar upgrade. Its LH90 and LH100 throttles can be upgraded to V3.6 by either changing the PROM yourself or by sending it to Lenz. Soon, you'll be able to upgrade the LVZ100 command station to an LVZ200 by sending it to Lenz. Once

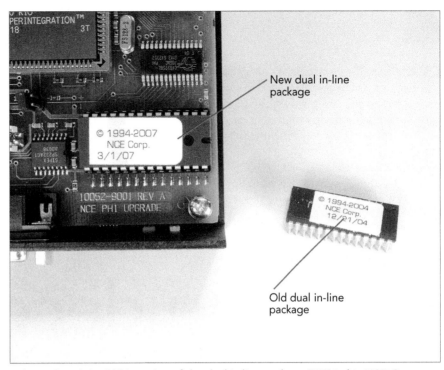

Mike replaced the 2004 version of the dual in-line package (DIP) in his NCE Corp. DCC throttle with one from 2007. The DIP can usually be removed with a small screwdriver, but work carefully to avoid bending the pins.

the system has an LVZ200, the end user can do further upgrades. These upgrades provide additional features such as bidirectional communication.

MRC offers manufacturer upgrades for its V1 wireless throttles and receivers to V2. All of the wireless components must be the same revision to work correctly together.

You can update NCE wireless throttles for improved performance by sending them in to the manufacturer to get the Generation 3 Radio upgrade. Downloadable firmware to upgrade Zimo's command station has been available for many years.

Decoders

In addition to throttles and command stations, decoders can be upgraded. Many times this can be done while the decoder is still in the locomotive, but it often requires a specialized programmer. These programmers can also be used for adjusting Configuration Variables in the decoder.

Digitrax's SoundFX decoders are an example of such a decoder. By use of either the PR2 or PR3 computer interface, you can download new sounds and update the decoder's firmware.

The Lenz Digital Plus Decoder Programmer lets you upgrade your Lenz decoders if they are already at least Revision 7 firmware.

Many factory sound-equipped locomotives use QS Industries decoders. QSI Solutions, a company that offers aftermarket QSI products, has upgrade chips for QSI decoders used in many Broadway Limited, InterMountain, Lionel HO, and Proto 2000 locomotives. Once the chips are updated to Revision 7, further upgrades can be accomplished with the Quantum Programmer.

Zimo decoders can be upgraded with the MXDECUP module, MX31ZL cab, or the MX10 command station.

By upgrading your DCC components, you can take advantage of additional features not offered when your system was designed and correct functional errors found and fixed after you purchased your system. For many years, replacement PROMs have been available, but more and more downloadable firmware and programmers are becoming available. This protects your investment in DCC equipment from becoming obsolete.

Installing decoders

Although there are an amazing number of locomotives on the market today with factory-installed decoders, odds are pretty good that you have engines in your fleet with 8-, 9-, or 21-pin sockets for a decoder, a motor isolated from the frame, or no provisions for DCC at all.

If you have locomotives in the latter categories, then Chapter 3 is right up your alley. We'll look at variety of projects, such as a installing a motor decoder in a 9-pin plug, using an N scale decoder in an HO locomotive, and adding two decoders to a brass steam locomotive. In addition, we'll explore how to install a decoder in an N scale model with an isolated frame (including tips on milling the frame), how to wire decoders in older Athearn diesels, and how to get decoder installations right on the first try.

Installing decoders right the first time

There's little in life that's more frustrating than having to do a job over again because it wasn't done right the first time. Here's what you can do to install a Digital Command Control (DCC) decoder properly the first time.

Research

There are many locomotives available today, with dozens of different available decoders. To find out which decoder is a good fit for your locomotive, search manufacturers' websites. Many sites have reference charts with specific locomotive references. (See page 34 for more info on choosing decoders.) Newer locomotives often have plug-and-play or drop-in decoders that make the installation easier. You can also ask in the DCC and Electronics forum at ModelRailroader.com or any of the Yahoo groups devoted to DCC.

There are many factors to consider when choosing a decoder. Foremost is motor current, which is the decoder's ability to accommodate the locomotive's motor current draw.

Also consider the number of functions the decoder offers. There must be enough functions to meet your locomotive lighting needs.

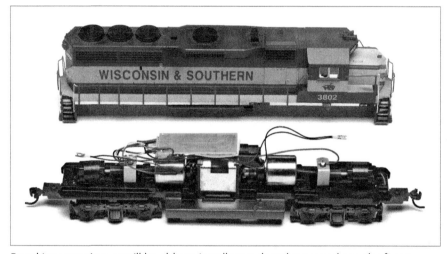

By taking your time, you'll be able to install your decoder properly on the first try. *Bill Zuback photos*

Check the physical size of the decoder. It must fit in the space available under the locomotive or tender shell.

If you want sound, you'll want to find a decoder with sounds appropriate for your locomotive, plus a space within the locomotive's shell for a speaker.

Lastly, think about any special features that you'd like your decoder to have. Do you want back-electromotive-force control, advanced consisting, or programmable speed tables? The list of features is seemingly endless.

Tools and supplies

Many tools make decoder installations easier. You'll need the basics shown in **1**: jeweler's screwdrivers, small needle-nose pliers, wire strippers for wire from 22AWG to 30AWG, a good 25-watt soldering iron (*not* a large soldering gun), and a multimeter capable of measuring voltage (up to 20V), resistance (ohms), and current (amps).

I also keep handy an assortment of color-coded wire, resistors, double-sided foam tape, electrical tape, heat-

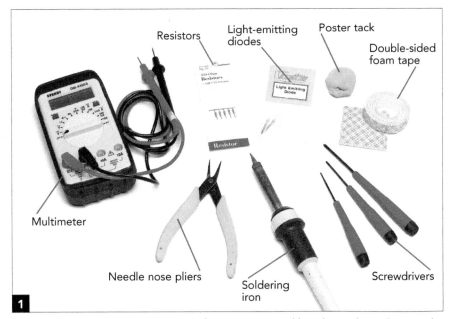

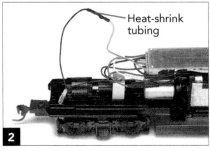

To prevent short circuits, cover wire joints with heat-shrink tubing. The tubing is available in various sizes.

1 Many of the items Mike recommends for your DCC workbench are shown here, and most are available at hobby shops and electronics stores. The poster tack and foam tape are in the office supply aisle at major retailers.

shrink tubing, poster putty, light bulbs, and light-emitting diodes.

Testing and planning

Test each decoder before installing it. If you install a decoder without testing it first and the locomotive doesn't work, what's the problem? Is it the decoder or your installation? If you then take the decoder out and test it, and it doesn't work, how do you know you didn't damage it?

There are many decoder testers on the market, and it's easy to build your own. Before I bought a commercial tester, I made my own using an old locomotive motor and some grain-of-wheat bulbs. It was a simple matter of connecting everything with test clips to see if the motor moved and the lights turned on.

Plan the installation carefully. Before you start, determine exactly where to place the decoder, how long the wires need to be, what kind of lighting you're going to use and where it will go, how you'll mount the decoder in the locomotive, and where the speaker (if any) will go. This is especially true if you need to cut or modify the frame.

Also determine if the motor is electrically isolated. The motor contacts must be completely isolated from the frame and/or wheels of the locomotive.

Work slowly and carefully. Like many of you, I get eager to see my finished, decoder-equipped locomotive move down the tracks. But with decoder installations, patience is critical. If part of the frame needs to be removed, cut off small pieces and test fit the decoder often. If you're cutting metal, remove the motor, gears, and decoder so you won't get shavings in them.

If you're using a heat gun on the heat-shrink tubing, remove items that might get damaged. The locomotive shell, plastic handrails, and the decoder can be damaged by excessive heat.

Cover conductive surfaces

I protect all wire joints with heat-shrink tubing to prevent short circuits, **2**. I've found the tubing works better for joints than electrical tape.

Many decoders have exposed circuitry, and the backs of some printed-circuit (PC) boards are uncovered. I put a piece of electrical tape on the back of the PC board or on the locomotive frame if it has any chance of touching an uncovered wire.

Some decoders are encased with heat-shrink or other tubing. Don't cover a decoder with tubing unless the manufacturer specifically states that you can. The tubing may cause the decoder to overheat.

Test during installation

This not only applies to test fitting the mechanical portion of the installation, but the electrical side as well. If you've modified the frame or track connections, test them with your multimeter to make sure there are connections where you want them and no shorts where you don't want them.

The first decoder connections I usually make are to the motor and the track. Once those are done, I can test the wiring by trying to read back the short address on my DCC system's programming track. I keep the locomotive on my bench and run test clips between its wheels and the programming track. The programming track has less current available than the main line. If there's a mistake, the chances of damaging the decoder are lower on the programming track. This is also great time to program the decoder to the address you want.

Then I wire and test the lighting and, if equipped, the speaker. These have to be tested on the main line. I have the programming track and main-line terminals connected to a rotary switch so I can connect either one to my test clips.

When you're completely satisfied with the testing, reassemble the locomotive and test it again. This time you can do it right on the layout. Pay close attention around curves and grades to make sure there aren't mechanical problems or short circuits caused by swiveling trucks.

If you're new to wiring and DCC, try a drop-in or plug-and-play decoder before you tackle a wired installation. As your knowledge and skills increase, attempt more advanced installations.

6 tips for buying a DCC decoder

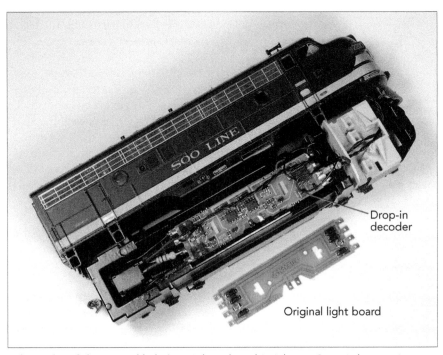

Drop-in decoder

Original light board

Mike replaced the original light/circuit board on this Athearn Genesis locomotive with a drop-in circuit-board-style decoder.

There are many options for DCC decoders today. Choosing the correct one may seem a little daunting, but it's easier than you think if you follow these six tips.

1 The right fit. It might seem obvious, but the first consideration when purchasing a decoder is finding one that will fit in the locomotive. Where it goes, however, might not be as obvious.

There are numerous drop-in (or plug-and-play) decoders available for just about every locomotive model manufactured in the past two decades. This type of decoder usually replaces the locomotive's light board and is often the best choice. However, in some cases the decoder is designed for all locomotive models from a particular manufacturer. I've sometimes found that slight modification to the

motor mounts or the locomotive's shell is necessary. Usually it's not difficult. Just take your time and make sure the decoder will fit.

Another type of plug-and-play decoder uses an 8- or 9-pin plug. Many locomotives, especially those advertised as DCC ready, have a receptacle for one plug or the other. Typically there's a dummy plug in the light board that you remove before installing the new plug.

Decoders equipped with plugs often have a 9-pin plug attached directly to the body and a removable harness that has a 9-pin plug on one side and an 8-pin plug on the other. If the locomotive has an 8-pin receptacle, it's a simple matter to plug in that harness. If it has a 9-pin receptacle, the decoder will plug directly into it. Separate 9-pin to 9-pin harnesses are also available.

Plug-equipped decoders come in all shapes and sizes, so you have a good

chance of finding one that will fit in your locomotive. I find it best to carefully measure the available space with calipers before trying to install the decoder. If you install the decoder in the locomotive without measuring first, the shell may not seat properly.

If a drop-in or plug-and-play decoder isn't available for your locomotive, or there isn't a decoder with the features that you want, you may choose to hard-wire your own. You can hardwire decoders with an 8- or 9-pin harness by cutting off the plug. Hardwiring a decoder gives you the freedom to place the decoder where it fits best. In several N scale locomotives, I've had to remove parts of the locomotive's weight for the decoder to fit properly. You may also consider installing the decoder in the cab or fuel tank of a diesel. On a steam locomotive, you can try placing it in the smokebox, cab, or tender. Again, careful measurement and planning is key to a successfully installation.

2 Current draw. It's equally important that the decoder is capable of supplying enough current for the locomotive's motor. Decoders have a motor stall current rating, which has to be greater than the current your locomotive actually draws when stalled. Measure the locomotive's stall current before converting it to DCC by placing an ammeter in series with a DC power pack and pushing down the locomotive until it stalls just long enough to make the measurement.

In reality, most decoders made for a particular scale can easily handle the current of a locomotive in that scale. Most HO locomotives draw well under 1A; N scale locomotives draw less than 750mA. Sometimes it's even possible to use an N scale decoder in an HO locomotive.

3 **Motor control.** There are several different motor control features available in today's DCC decoders. Low-speed control can be accomplished by several different techniques, such as back-electromotive-force control (back-EMF).

Decoder manufacturers have different methods for implementing back-EMF. Because of this, fine-tuning of the decoder may be necessary. Some decoders use different Configuration Variables (CVs) to control back-EMF, while in others it's automatic. Until you are comfortable adjusting back-EMF, I recommend using the same brand of decoder or disabling back-EMF.

Some decoders have other methods to provide low-speed control. These usually involve variable duration and variable voltage pulses to the motor, both of which can be quite effective.

Besides low-speed control, it's usually desirable for consisted locomotives to run at the same speed at a given throttle setting. There are two methods for speed matching locomotives. The first is through the use of CVs for Vstart, Vmax, and Vmid. By adjusting these CVs, you can set the voltage at throttle step 0, mid-throttle, and maximum throttle.

The second way to speed match locomotives is with speed tables. These are a series of CVs that set the voltage at each throttle step. When speed tables are enabled, the other speed control CVs are disabled. Speed tables take a bit more time to set up, but they typically do a better job of speed matching.

Not all decoders offer both methods of speed matching. The National Model Railroad Association only requires the Vstart CV. Some decoders only have Vstart and the ability to use a speed table. Others don't use speed tables. I recommend using the same method of speed matching for all of your locomotives.

4 **Lighting functions.** Locomotives equipped with DCC can dazzle you with lighting effects that weren't possible with DC locomotives of the past. If this is important to you, make sure that the decoder you choose has enough functions to light everything you want.

Prototype diesels have headlights at each end, illuminated number boxes, cab lights, ditch lights, ground lights, step lights, beacons, oscillating headlights, and Mars lights, among other lights. Most decoders have programmable lighting effects for just about every one of these, but the number of available lighting functions can be limited.

If you use an 8-pin plug, only the front and rear headlights and one other function can be used. Often only the forward and reverse headlights are wired. Decoders with a 9-pin plug can have a total of four lighting functions, but they may not all be wired. A decoder with an 8-pin plug often has an extra wire from the decoder that can be hardwired for an additional light.

5 **Sound.** One of the biggest advancements in decoders offered in smaller scales is sound. Some modelers prefer the exact sound for the locomotive's prime mover as well as the correct bell and horn for a particular railroad. Others are content with generic locomotive sound effects.

There's such a variety in sound decoders that it may take some time to find one that has the correct sounds and features you want. Regardless of the features you want, volume control is essential. Make sure there is an individual control for each sound effect.

Manufacturers list the different sound decoders they offer on their websites. If a decoder isn't available with the sounds that you need, recommend it to the manufacturer. There's no guarantee it will be made, but odds are if you need it, other modelers do too.

6 **Resources.** *Model Railroader* publishes decoder reviews and feature articles on decoder installation, and the DCC Corner column often gives how-to information on decoders. Even if the installation isn't for your exact locomotive, the articles might help you decide which decoder you'd like.

Your local hobby shop may install decoders and may have some advice for you as well. Even if the shop doesn't install decoders, the store owner or

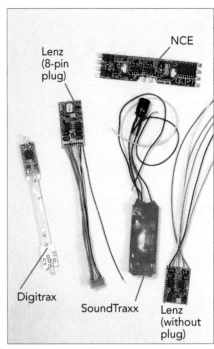

This photo shows the various shapes and sizes of Digital Command Control decoders, including drop-in style and those with and without plugs. Other manufacturers include Model Rectifier Corp., Train Control Systems, and ESU.

shop employees may be able to provide input based on what they've been selling to (and hearing from) customers.

Decoder manufacturer websites have a wealth of information, including recommended decoders for a locomotive, installation photos, lists of available sounds, and—perhaps the most useful—manuals for each decoder. Reading a manual or two will give you a good idea of a decoder's features. After you narrow your selection, you can read the complete decoder manual before purchasing the decoder to make sure it's the one you want.

There are also Internet discussion groups for almost every type of DCC interest. Chances are someone has tried the decoder installation you are attempting. Group etiquette is to check the archives for the answer to your question prior to posting a question.

With so many decoders to pick from, it's easy to understand why modelers get nervous when making this big purchase. But if you keep these six tips in mind, your next decoder purchase will be a far less nerve-wracking event.

How to replace a bad decoder

By Cody Grivno

A bad decoder didn't mean the end of the road for Milwaukee, Racine & Troy no. 1100. *Model Railroader* associate editor Cody Grivno replaced the model's factory-installed decoder with a 6-function decoder. *Jim Forbes photos*

I'd just put the finishing touches on Milwaukee, Racine & Troy no. 1100, an Atlas HO scale General Electric Dash 8-40B that I painted and decaled for the July 2011 issue of *Model Railroader*. The model came with a dual-mode 4-function decoder. I moved the jumper plug from analog to DCC and set the engine on our club layout to give it a test run. After I turned on the layout power, I heard a small pop, caught a whiff of singed electronics, and saw a wisp of smoke.

This unit didn't come with a smoke unit, so I knew something was wrong. I removed the shell and confirmed that the decoder was shot. I didn't want the freshly painted locomotive to be relegated to a showcase piece, so I had to find a fix.

Because this is an older Atlas model, an exact replacement motor

decoder wasn't available. While looking around for a suitable replacement, I came across the Train Control Systems A6X. The 6-function decoder features back-electromotive-force control and onboard current-limit resistors. It can be used with models that have 1.5 and 12V bulbs and light-emitting diodes.

Swapping circuit boards

Replacing the factory printed-circuit (PC) board with the A6X is an easy project that can be completed in an evening. First, I removed the two Phillips screws that hold the PC board with the jumper plug. Then I removed the plastic retainers that secure the wires to the dual-mode decoder. After the wires were free, I gently squeezed the plastic tabs with a straight-slot screwdriver to release the larger PC board, **1**.

The A6X has slots that line up perfectly with the plastic tabs above the Dash 8's motor. After gently snapping the board into place, I attached the front and rear power pickup wires to their appropriate soldering pads. Though I could have secured the wires with the plastic retainers from the Atlas model, I soldered the wires to the pads for a more reliable connection.

Since the wires aren't color coded, make sure you have the correct wire for the pad before soldering the connection. Although I didn't do it here, you could paint the wires to match National Model Railroad Association standards.

Next, I soldered the motor wires to their pads following the wiring diagram included with the decoder. The red wire goes to the right pad and the black wire to the left.

Finally, I wired the headlights. This is where some extra work is required. I soldered the red wires to their respective pads on the end of the PC board. The black wire for the rear headlight is long enough to reach the small pad indicated in **2**. However, I had to lengthen the black wire for the front headlight.

To make the wire long enough to reach the soldering pad, I made a Western Union splice. First, I stripped insulation from a second piece of wire (the insulation was already stripped from the wire connected to the LED). Then I made a 90-degree bend in each piece of wire and hooked the two lengths together. Finally, I twisted the wires tightly around each other, **3**.

When it came time to solder the splice, I applied rosin soldering flux paste to the splice. Then I held the tip of the soldering iron so it heated both wires and applied 60/40 rosin-core solder from the opposite side. Once the

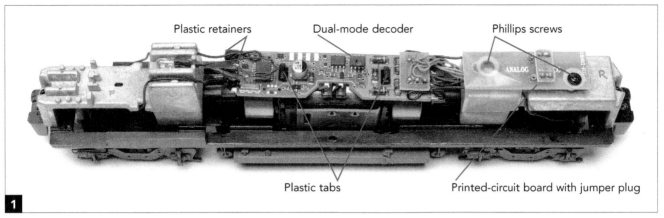

1

Plastic retainers   Dual-mode decoder   Phillips screws

Plastic tabs   Printed-circuit board with jumper plug

The Atlas Dash 8-40B came with a factory-installed 4-function decoder. The assembly was held on with two Phillips screws and two plastic tabs.

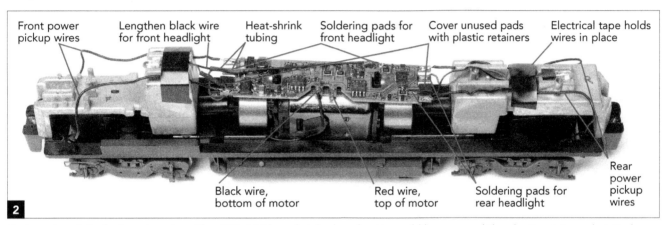

2

Front power pickup wires   Lengthen black wire for front headlight   Heat-shrink tubing   Soldering pads for front headlight   Cover unused pads with plastic retainers   Electrical tape holds wires in place

Black wire, bottom of motor   Red wire, top of motor   Soldering pads for rear headlight   Rear power pickup wires

Cody replaced the factory decoder with a TCS A6X board-style decoder. He could have reused the plastic retainers, but Cody chose to solder the wires to the pads for greater reliability.

splice looked wet, I removed the solder, and then the iron. The solder should be bright and shiny. If it has a frosted or dull appearance, you have a cold joint that won't provide a reliable electrical connection.

Before attaching the wire to the soldering pad, I applied a piece of heat-shrink tubing. Since the splice is over the PC board, this will prevent an accidental short circuit.

A heat gun is a popular way to shrink the tubing, but it seemed too risky here. Instead, I held a hot soldering iron near the tubing. Though a soldering iron doesn't shrink the tube as neatly as a heat gun, it was far less likely to damage the plastic parts.

I tested the decoder on our club layout before reassembling the locomotive. Thankfully there was no pop, smell of burnt electronics, or smoke. The locomotive ran in both directions, and the headlights worked as advertised. I then set the decoder's address to

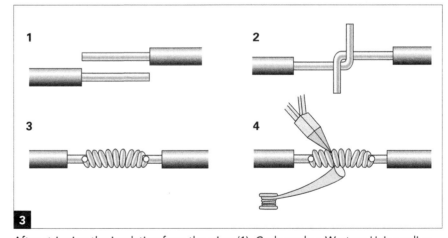

3

After stripping the insulation from the wires (1), Cody made a Western Union splice by bending the wires at a 90-degree angle (2), twisting the wires tightly around each other (3), and soldering the splice (4). *Rick Johnson illustration*

1100 following the steps on our Model Rectifier Corp. Prodigy Advanced DCC throttle.

Finally, I used electrical tape to neatly hold the wires in place. This not only keeps the wires from getting tangled in moving parts, but it makes it

easier to seat the shell properly.

Once the shell was in place, I installed the two draft-gear boxes and screwed them into the chassis. With that, no. 1100 can resume its duties as the class locomotive of the MR&T's Dash-8 fleet.

Add a decoder to a Kato N scale SD45

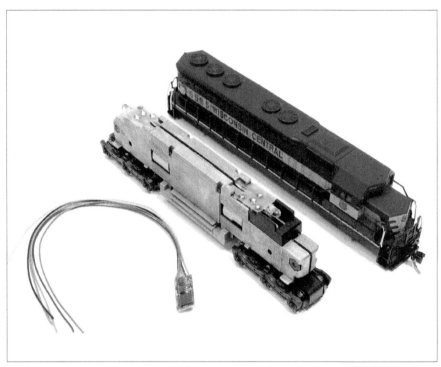

Mike explains how he installed a non-plug Train Control Systems decoder in this older version of a Kato N scale SD45.

My son, Matt, had an older Kato N scale SD45 that needed a decoder. Newer runs of this locomotive have a single light board, and drop-in decoders are available. This one, however, has two small light boards, one at each end, requiring a hard-wired decoder.

After I tested the locomotive on DC to make sure it ran correctly, I removed the press-fit shell to see what was inside. The SD45 uses a split-frame mechanism, with each half connected through the trucks to the rails. The motor brushes are attached to each side of the frame via brass contacts. To install a decoder, I had to isolate the brushes from the frame.

I soon discovered that about the only place for a decoder was inside the fuel tank, which was completely filled with the metal frame. Aztec Manufacturing (www.aztectrains.com) offers a frame milling service for the Kato SD45 and other N scale locomotives. If you send Aztec your frame, they'll mill out a section large enough to install a decoder.

I saved a little money and removed the metal myself using a motor tool and a cutoff disk. Before modifying the frame, I purchased a decoder so I knew exactly how much material to remove.

Frame modification

I chose the Z2 decoder from Train Control Systems (www.tcsdcc.com) because of its small size and good low-speed performance. However, any number of hard-wired decoders will work as long as they'll fit inside the model.

I started by testing the decoder prior to installation at my workbench to make sure it worked properly. After measuring the decoder, I marked the area of the frame that needed to be removed, **1**. Before cutting the frame, I completely disassembled the locomotive.

Cutting the frame is a messy procedure and metal filings should be kept away from the motor, trucks, gears, bearings, and decoder. Study how the locomotive is assembled before taking it apart, and make any necessary notes to ensure proper reassembly.

I clamped half the frame to my workbench. Then I cut along the outer edges of the marked area, working slowly and carefully. Be sure to wear proper eye protection. When I felt I was close to breaking through, I used a pair of needlenose pliers to rock the piece of metal back and forth until it broke free. You can see the finished opening in **1**. I repeated this process with the other half of the frame.

After I'd cut out both sides of the frame, I test-fit the decoder. Once I was satisfied with the fit, I filed the sharp edges. I also used a round file to shape a groove in the frame and notches in the motor carrier for routing wires, **2**. These notches prevent the wires from getting pinched going past the motor.

I finished work on the frame by using compressed air to blow away any loose metal filings. Then I washed the frame in water with a few drops of liquid dish soap added to remove the last of the filings. I let the frame dry overnight before reassembling the locomotive.

Reassembly

I reassembled the locomotive a little at a time, making sure I had a clear path for the wires. I started by cutting the orange and gray wires to length and

1

Mike used a marker to indicate where he'd need to cut the metal frame, as shown in the left photo. At right, you can see where Mike used a motor tool with a cutoff disk to cut the metal frame. Proper eye protection is a must when using a cutoff disk.

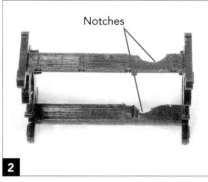

Notches

2

To prevent the wires from getting pinched against the motor, Mike used a round file to shape notches in the motor carrier for routing the wires.

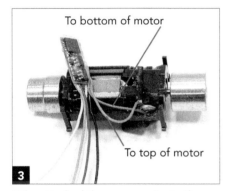

To bottom of motor

To top of motor

3

Mike attached the orange wire to the top motor brush and the gray wire to the bottom one.

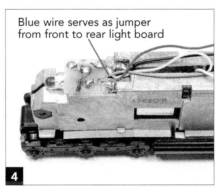

Blue wire serves as jumper from front to rear light board

4

After attaching the yellow wire to the rear light board, Mike used a length of blue wire to connect the front light board to the back.

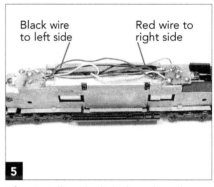

Black wire to left side

Red wire to right side

5

After installing the light boards and diodes, Mike made the final wire connections. The extra red and black connections give the locomotive redundant contact paths.

soldering them to the brass contacts that connect the frame to the motor, **3**. Make sure the joint is as flat as possible. Large blobs of solder can prevent the motor from seating properly in the frame.

It's also important that the electrical connections are completely covered in heat-shrink tubing. If they contact the frame, the decoder will be destroyed. As a precaution, I lined the inside of the motor cavity with electrical tape.

I routed the yellow, black, red, white, and blue wires to the top of the frame. Once I'd reassembled the two sides of the frame, I worked on the light boards.

There's a light board at each end of the locomotive with a light-emitting diode (LED) headlight and a current-limiting resistor. The power for the lights comes from contacts wedged into slots in the frame. This is where I got the power for the decoder's red

and black wires. Next, using a sharp knife, I cut the traces on the printed-circuit (PC) board, isolating the LED and resistor from the power contacts. I left enough of the traces to attach the headlight wires.

On the front light board, I attached the white wire to the right side, making sure the resistor was in series with the LED. I repeated the process with the back light board, this time attaching the yellow wire, **4**. I used a section of blue wire left over from another installation as a jumper across from the front light board to the back.

Finally, I soldered the red wire to the contact that wedges into the frame on the right side of the locomotive and the black wire to the left side. I used black and red wires to connect these contacts to the front to the back light boards. It's not necessary to put in these connections, but I found these redundant paths make the locomotive

more reliable. You can see the finished wiring in **5**.

I tested the installation by placing the locomotive on my programming track and reading back CV1, the short address. All decoders come factory programmed to address 3. I programmed the long address to 6585 (the road number) and activated the long address in CV29.

I then placed the locomotive on the main line and ran it back and forth. Should the locomotive run opposite of the throttle setting, you can either reverse the orange and gray wires or add 1 to the default value already programmed into CV29.

This decoder installation took about three evenings to complete. Using an Aztec milled frame certainly would have saved some effort, but cutting the frame myself wasn't that difficult. Just work carefully and wear proper safety gear.

Most any decoder will do in a pinch

By David Popp

The techniques shown here on a Bachmann FM will work on other models with split-frame construction.

The *Model Railroader* staff had some diesel locomotives in need of DCC decoders for our HO scale Virginian project railroad, which began appearing in the January 2012 issue. We had purchased a pair of Bachmann Fairbanks-Morse H16-44 diesels for the railroad, so I set to work on installing decoders in them.

I was a bit pushed for time on the project, so I checked with Cody Grivno, MR's "new product guy," to see what we had on hand for decoders. He gave me several Train Control Systems (TCS) drop-in decoders designed for InterMountain N scale FT locomotives. With four functions, back-electromotive-force (BEMF) control, and a rating of 1A continuous and 2A peak draw, the small printed-circuit-board decoders would work well for the Bachmann H16-44s.

Wait—HO locomotives with N scale drop-in decoders? Rest assured that these little decoders are a good fit for this project. They screw into the top of the engine shell, replacing the original light board, and all of the soldering pads are easy to reach, making them easy to wire. In fact, as long as it can handle the current and function requirements of the model, nearly any decoder can do in a pinch—and with a deadline looming, a pinch was exactly what I faced!

The project was straightforward. I needed to completely disassemble the models, and the fact that the engines are held together with screws made them easy to take them apart. The first installation took me an hour and a half. I proceeded carefully, marked everything clearly, and tested my work often as I went—all of which paid off with a model that worked correctly the first time. Once I knew what I was doing, the second locomotive went quickly.

As long as you can isolate the motor, you can use this decoder and the following process with many other models.

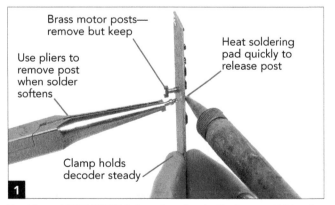

David used TCS IMFTA4 decoders for the Bachmann Fairbanks-Morse diesels. These come with brass contact posts that protrude through the back of the decoder. To remove the posts, he heated the mounting pads with a soldering iron and pulled the post free. *Jim Forbes photos*

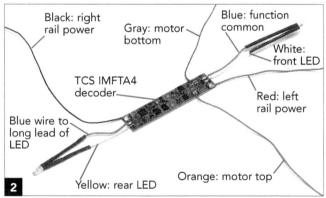

All connections to the decoder are made using soldering pads. The decoder is equipped with resistors for use with light-emitting diodes (LEDs), so David replaced the model's 12V bulbs with 3mm RL3-W8030 white LEDs from www.superbrightleds.com.

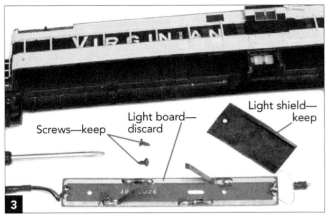

3

Screws—keep
Light board—discard
Light shield—keep

The locomotive is held together with a number of screws, making it very easy to disassemble the model. David removed and discarded the lighting circuit board; however, he kept the screws and the paper light shield to be used again later when reassembling the model.

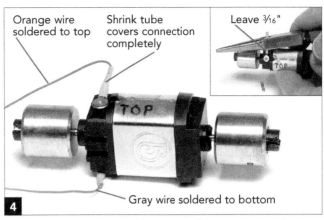

4

Orange wire soldered to top
Shrink tube covers connection completely
Leave 3/16"
TOP
Gray wire soldered to bottom

David marked the top of the motor before removing it from the frame. The motor uses brass wipers to collect power from the frame, and he clipped these off, leaving 3/16", which he used as soldering pads to attach the motor wires. He covered the connections with shrink tube.

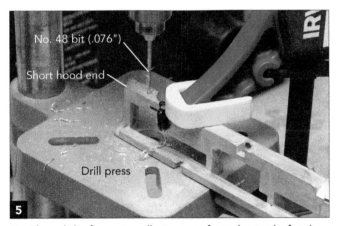

5

No. 48 bit (.076")
Short hood end
Drill press

David used the frame to collect power from the trucks for the decoder. After removing the motor and trucks, he drilled a hole on the short-hood end of both halves of the frame with a no. 48 bit. David placed a drop of oil on the tip of the bit before drilling to make the job easier.

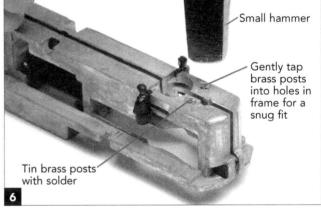

6

Small hammer
Gently tap brass posts into holes in frame for a snug fit
Tin brass posts with solder

For frame contacts, David used the decoder's brass posts, which are .076" at their widest point. He slightly widened the entrance to the holes with a reamer, then placed the posts in the holes and tapped them home with a hammer. Next, he tinned the tops with solder.

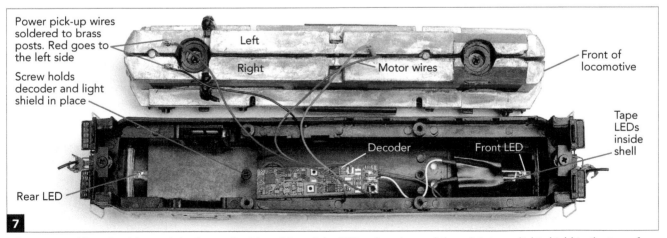

7

Power pick-up wires soldered to brass posts. Red goes to the left side
Left
Right
Motor wires
Front of locomotive
Screw holds decoder and light shield in place
Decoder
Front LED
Tape LEDs inside shell
Rear LED

After reassembling the drive and the frame, David positioned the LEDs, decoder, and the cab's paper light shield in the top of the shell. A single screw holds almost everything in place, although David used some electrical tape to attach the front LED. Next, he soldered the power pickup wires to the brass frame contacts (red wire to the left half). He then replaced the shell on the chassis and tested the work with the MR workshop's DCC system. Working carefully and marking the motor paid off, as it all functioned smoothly on the first attempt!

Add two decoders to a brass locomotive

Mike explains how he added motor and sound decoders to a brass model of a Soo Line 2-8-0.

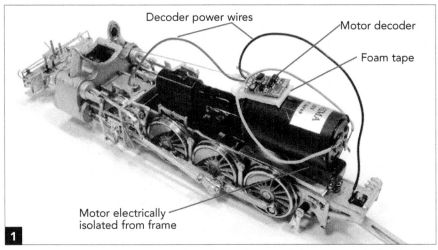

Mike attached the Lenz Silver Mini decoder to the top of the motor with double-sided foam tape. He put electrical tape on the inner surface of the boiler to prevent a short circuit.

I have a number of older brass steam locomotives that I want to update with DCC and sound. You can follow how I added two decoders—one for the motor and one for sound—to a Samhongsa Soo Line 2-8-0, and apply the same methods to many other brass steam locomotives. Even though this 2-8-0 is an HO scale model, it has a relatively small boiler and an even smaller tender.

Many brass steam locomotives have room in the tender for a speaker and holes in the floor that allow the sound

to escape. The can motor is electrically isolated from the frame of this model, which helps when installing decoders.

The success of any decoder installation depends upon proper planning. The first thing I did was run the locomotive on DC to see if it operated well. It did, and I then measured how much current the motor drew: a scant 200 milliamps (mA; .200 amps).

I removed the three screws that hold the boiler to the frame. The first is a long screw that is under the frame

between the cylinders and extends up into the boiler. The other two are on the back of the locomotive under the cab. I was pleasantly surprised to find there was room between the inner surface of the boiler and the top of the motor for a small motor decoder.

Next, I removed the four screws that hold the tender to the body floor. I found I could fit a 1"-diameter speaker and a sound decoder inside.

Motor decoder

Although I was installing two decoders, I only needed one extra wire between the tender and the locomotive. Like most brass steam locomotive models, the tender picks up power from one rail and the locomotive from the other. The drawbar between the two carries the power from the tender to the locomotive's motor. With the extra wire, I could get the other rail's power back to the tender.

I used a Lenz Silver Mini motor decoder with back-electromotive-force control (back-EMF). This decoder has exceptional low-speed control and

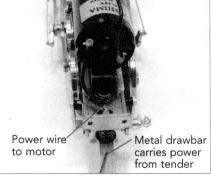

On the Samhongsa 2-8-0, two wires supply power to the motor. The left photo shows the first wire soldered to a screw above the front drivers. The right photo shows the second wire soldered to the screw that holds the sprung drawbar in place.

Speaker   Sound decoder

3

Mike inserted the speaker and enclosure in the rear of the tender. He used double-sided foam tape to hold the sound decoder in place.

4

This capacitor helps prevent power for the sounds from being interrupted if the locomotive crosses dirty rails.

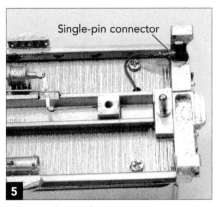

Single-pin connector

5

Mike used a single-pin connector to attach the red wire from the sound decoder to the black wire on the locomotive frame.

easily fit in the 2-8-0. It's capable of supplying 500mA, which is more than sufficient.

I attached the decoder to the top of the motor with double-sided foam tape, **1**. Since the boiler is also brass, I insulated the inside of the boiler with electrical tape to prevent a short circuit. Don't wrap the decoder in tape or heat-shrink tubing, as this may lead to overheating.

Two wires supply power to the motor. One is soldered to a screw above the front drivers, and the other is soldered to the screw that secures the drawbar, **2**. I unsoldered these wires and soldered the red decoder wire to the screw attached to the frame. I attached the black wire to the drawbar screw.

On the 2-8-0, the frame picks up through the right-hand wheels and the tender from the left-hand. I soldered another wire to the frame to carry right-rail power back to the tender for the sound decoder. Even though this wire is connected to the locomotive frame and red wire, I used a black wire so it would be less obvious between the locomotive and the tender.

I soldered the orange and gray wires from the decoder to the motor terminals. If the locomotive had a headlight bulb, I would have attached it to the blue and white wires. I trimmed the unused wires and wrapped them with electrical tape.

Before reassembling the engine, I tested the motor decoder by placing the locomotive on my test track and clipping the drawbar to the left rail.

Before I ran the locomotive, I read back CV1 to see if the decoder was wired correctly.

Sound decoder

I chose a SoundTraxx Micro-Tsunami sound decoder, which has good sounds and fits neatly into the tender with the speaker. I wanted to use the largest speaker I could. A 1"-diameter speaker and enclosure from Tony's Train Exchange fit perfectly.

I first drilled a small hole in the side of the speaker enclosure and fed the purple wires through the hole and soldered them to the speaker terminals. I attached the decoder under the coal bunker with double-sided foam tape. I then inserted the speaker into the enclosure and attached the decoder to the top of the inside of the tender with the foam tape, **3**. I soldered the black wire from the decoder to the inside of the tender floor. Finally, I drilled a hole into the tender floor so I could route the red wire through the opening.

SoundTraxx supplies an optional (but highly desirable) capacitor to keep the sound decoder from cutting out over dirty rails. Since I had room for the capacitor, I soldered the negative side (with the stripe) to the green/yellow wire and the positive side to the blue wire, **4**.

I tested the sound decoder by placing the tender on my test track and attaching the red wire to the right rail. I then connected the main line to the test track and selected address 3. I sounded the whistle and bell and ran the throttle

through its range of speed steps.

I used a small single-pin connector to link the red wire from the sound decoder with the black wire attached to the locomotive frame. I cemented the female side of the connector to the tender floor with cyanoacrylate adhesive, **5**, and soldered the red wire to it. I soldered the black wire from the locomotive to the male side.

I tested both decoders by attaching the tender to the locomotive and connecting the extra wire between the two. It's important to remember that there are now two decoders programmed to the same address. Because they're both on the test track, configuration variables (CVs) of the same number in both decoders will be programmed at the same time. Other than the address, none of the CVs I needed to program overlapped.

I adjusted the chuff rate of the sound decoder to match the speed of the Lenz motor decoder. I found that by programming CV116 on the sound decoder to 20, I was able to get 4 chuffs per revolution at slow speeds.

Then I selected the appropriate whistle. I found that programming CV115 to number 1 gave me a whistle close to those on restored Soo Line locomotives.

By planning the installation beforehand and taking my time, installing the motor and sound decoders in my brass 2-8-0 went smoothly and turned out to be an enjoyable project. You can use many of these techniques for your favorite brass steam locomotive.

4 easy installations and 1 near miss

By David Popp

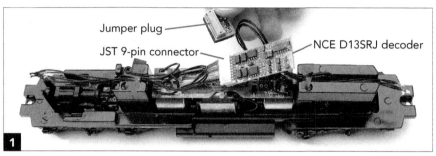

1

For Athearn models featuring a "Quick Plug," use a decoder with a JST 9-pin connector. Simply remove the small jumper circuit board, plug in a decoder with a JST connector, and you're ready to program the engine. *Bill Zuback photos*

Recently, after doing some much-needed cleaning of our Milwaukee, Racine & Troy HO club layout, we discovered that we had far more locomotives waiting for the installation of decoders than we had DCC-equipped engines on the layout. And, of the DCC-equipped locomotives we did have, most had early, no-frills decoders in them—those without advanced consisting, back-electromotive-force control, or programmable lighting effects.

So, after doing some quick decoder shopping, one Friday afternoon Neil Besougloff, Cody Grivno, Kent Johnson, and I took over most of the benches in the *Model Railroader* workshop and set up what is now known as "the great MR&T fleet overhaul." Thanks to the ease of installation provided by many of the newer decoders, we cranked out more than a dozen engines in just a couple of hours.

Installation

The locomotives equipped with JST 9-pin connectors were the simplest to work on. These include Athearn models that come with factory-installed "Quick Plugs." Many manufacturers make decoders with JST connectors, and we used NCE D13SRJ decoders for some of our Athearn SD40-2s and a C44-9W model.

As shown in **1**, we removed the jumper plug from the JST connector (gentle prying with a screwdriver helped release the part) and then installed the decoder. It actually took longer to remove the shell than to convert the engine to DCC. When reassembling the model, be sure that the decoder is seated properly and that it doesn't touch metal parts, or it may cause a short circuit.

While we were at it, we also swapped out decoders in a few of our vintage MR&T engines. Andy Sperandeo had wired several SD40-2s with harnesses that included JST 9-pin connectors, so upgrading these locomotives was just as easy as the Quick Plug engines.

The rest of our SD40-2 fleet needed to have the decoders wired in. For a detailed explanation of the process, see the June 2007 *Model Railroader*, but photo **2** shows most of the basics. The NCE D13SRJ decoders come with a wiring harness attached to the JST 9-pin connector, so we used the same decoder for this installation as well.

The key to success is to have good soldering points on the locomotive frame for a solid electrical connection. We drilled and tapped the frame so we could install a 1-72 brass screw, **2**. We then soldered the black track power

wire to the screw. Although they aren't shown in the photo, we equipped these locomotives with headlights using Miniatronics no. 1801410 14V bulbs.

Sound

Our commuter train fleet is powered by several Kato F40PH locomotives, and Digitrax makes a drop-in sound decoder (SDH164K1C) specifically for these engines. The decoder replaces the model's printed-circuit board and includes LED headlights and a speaker.

To replace the Kato PC board, I first removed the two screws that held it to the locomotive's chassis. I then gently slipped the two metal track-power tabs from either side of the board and carefully pulled the board free from the motor contact posts. To install the decoder, I reversed the process. Take extra care when inserting the motor contact posts into the decoder's circuit board, as these parts can be damaged easily.

Next, I snapped the speaker into the plastic enclosure, **3**, that is part of the F40PH's shell and slipped the speaker's capacitor under the rear light bar. As a final step, I clipped off the unused function wires to keep them from getting tangled in the locomotive's drive mechanism.

Atlas upgrade

For the MR&T's sizeable collection of Atlas GP38 and Dash 8-40B locomotives, we replaced the older Atlas circuit board decoders with Train Control Systems (TCS) A4X decoders. These decoders are made to be a direct swap (no soldering), and are used with locomotives that have 14V headlight bulbs.

To remove the original circuit board, we slipped the plastic locking covers off of all 10 wire contacts and carefully detached the wires. The board is held to the chassis with two plastic tabs, and it's easy to remove. To complete the installation, we snapped the TCS decoder in place and then reconnected all of the wires. If you want a more secure connection, you can solder the wires instead of using the plastic covers.

Near miss

TCS also makes another version of the A4X decoder, called an A6X. This decoder has built-in resistors for use with 1.5V headlight bulbs, as found on Walthers Proto 2000 models, some Athearn engines, and others. (Yes, we learned this one the hard way.) This means that you don't need to figure out resistor values or solder resistors into the light circuit when installing a decoder.

Even though we all knew we should have checked the bulb values ahead of time, we attempted to replace the circuit board on an Athearn SD70M with an A4X decoder, which resulted in blowing the front headlights. We then wisely replaced the A4X with an A6X, installing two new 1.5V bulbs in the process. We learned our lesson, so our other SD70s will all get A6X decoders from the start.

The SD70s include ditch lights, so we soldered the leads for those to the decoder's green and purple pads, **4**. Easy-to-follow programming instructions for the ditch lights are on the TCS website.

Basic programming

When programming a locomotive with a new decoder for the first time, I start by checking its address using a programming track. If I can read back the decoder's default address (3), that usually means the decoder is installed properly. I then program the locomotive's new address to match its road number.

Next, I set a couple of other basic configuration variables (CVs). For this step, I use programming on the main (ops mode) so I can quickly test the results and make changes if needed. First, I adjust the start voltage (CV2) so that the engine begins moving slowly at speed step 1 when using 128 speed steps. I start by programming

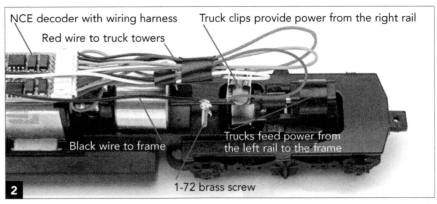

To make a solid solder connection between the decoder and the frame, the MR staff installed a 1-72 brass screw. The black wire connects to the frame and the red to both truck clips.

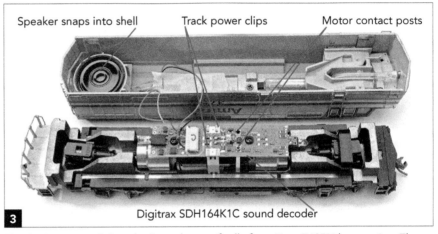

This Digitrax sound decoder is made specifically for a Kato F40PH locomotive. The model's motor contact posts and track power clips are delicate, so use care when attaching them to the decoder.

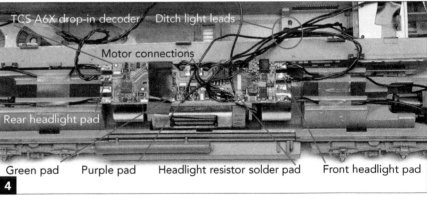

This Athearn SD70M locomotive comes with 1.5V headlight bulbs, so the MR staff used a TCS A6X decoder with a built-in resistor. One lead from each 1.5V bulb must be soldered to the resistor pad.

CV2 with a value of 35. If the engine moves too suddenly at speed step 1, I then reprogram CV2 with a lower value. If it doesn't move at step 1, I increase the value by increments of 5 until it does. I also put just a hint of momentum into the locomotive, using

CV3 (acceleration rate) and CV4 (deceleration rate). By adding a little momentum, it helps smooth out jerky starts and stops. I start with a value of 5 in each CV and test it along the way. If there isn't much change, then I try a value of 10 or 15.

Drop-in decoders for N scale diesels

By Eric White

This Proto N from Walthers GP20 will be one of the locomotives on a *Model Railroader* project layout. Read how associate editor Eric White installed a Digitrax DN163LOA drop-in decoder on this model. *MR Staff photos*

Among the projects facing the *Model Railroader* staff in preparing for a new N scale project layout was the task of installing decoders in two Proto N from Walthers GP20s. They're each getting a Digitrax DN163LOA drop-in decoder, designed to replace the light board in the GP20.

The first step is to remove the body shell. I pulled the fuel tank casting from the bottom of the unit, revealing the bottom of the split metal frame. I grasped this nub of frame and the body shell and gently pulled them apart.

I made sure to grab the body by the long hood and not the walkways. It took a fair amount of force to remove the shell from the frame. On the second model, I discovered I could use a small screwdriver to lever the frame from the body shell in the fuel tank area, **1**.

The model is a typical N scale design, with a motor and drivetrain sandwiched between two halves of a split zinc-alloy frame. The light board, **2**, is slotted into the top of the frame with contacts hanging down the sides to feed power to the motor. The light board collects power from the split frame with copper pads that wedge into slots in the top of the frame halves.

I removed the light board. There's a plastic shim under the board to keep it from moving around—remove it, **3**, before removing the light board.

The decoder board has two tabs at the front that make contact with the frame halves, **2**, and two copper tabs that supply power to the tabs on the motor. The original light board uses the same arrangement.

First, I had to protect the decoder from possible short circuits. I placed a piece of Kapton tape, **4**, on the top of the frame above the motor. Digitrax secures the decoder to a piece of foam for shipping with a piece of Kapton. For placement of the tape, I referred to both the printed instruction booklet that came with the decoder and the

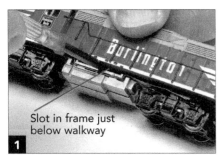

Slot in frame just below walkway

1. Eric used a screwdriver to help remove the body shell. It's difficult to grasp the long hood firmly, and the walkways are too fragile to pull on them.

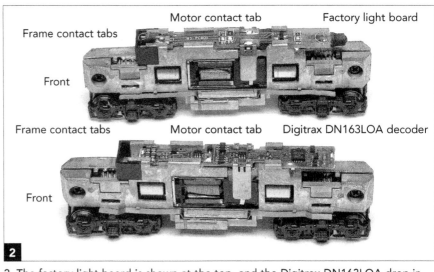

Motor contact tab — Factory light board — Frame contact tabs — Front — Frame contact tabs — Motor contact tab — Digitrax DN163LOA decoder — Front

2. The factory light board is shown at the top, and the Digitrax DN163LOA drop-in decoder is shown installed below.

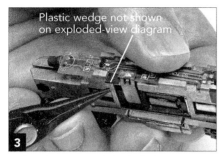

Before he removed the light board, Eric pulled out this wedge of plastic with a small pair of smooth-jaw, needlenose pliers. The shim keeps the factory light board from sliding around in the frame. It wasn't used for the decoder installation.

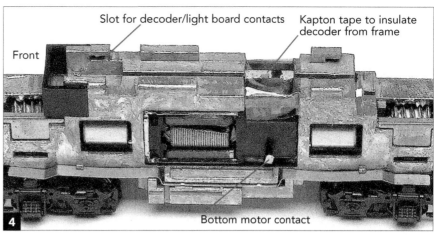

The frame is ready for the installation of the decoder. Make sure the bottom motor contact goes behind the decoder contact.

online instructions available at Digitrax's website, www.digitrax.com.

It's the same information, but it was easier to see the photos on my computer in color than to rely on the black-and-white copies on the printed instructions.

Once I had the tape in place, I slid the decoder into the tabs on the top of the frame, making sure the contacts from the motor were under the tabs from the decoder, and took the chassis to the programming track.

Troubleshooting

All done, right? Not quite.

When I put the first model on the track, I got, at best, intermittent performance from the decoder. The lights came on and blinked, and the model moved an inch or so, then stopped.

Checking continuity from the track through the frame showed the problem wasn't in the locomotive itself, but I noticed that when I moved the board on the frame, it worked a little better.

Even though the board fit tightly into the slots in the frame, the engine wasn't operating as well as it should. The problem was contact between the decoder and the frame. Senior editor Dana Kawala suggested two possible solutions.

The easy fix was to wedge a bit of plastic between the decoder and the frame, forcing the pads on the decoder into firmer contact with the frame. This helped some, but getting the wedge in exactly the right spot and keeping it there wasn't easy, and wasn't reliable.

The original shim wasn't in the right location to help with electrical contact, so I couldn't use that either.

The other option was to build up the pads on the decoder with a little bit of solder, making them thicker for better contact with the frame. Digitrax also makes this suggestion in its Mobile & Sound Decoder Manual, which is available online.

These circuit boards are tiny, so it only took a drop of solder to get the effect I wanted. Using a clean soldering iron, I put a bit of flux on the pad, then melted a drop of solder onto the tip of the soldering iron. When I touched the iron to the pad on the decoder, it deposited a drop of solder, **5**. I switched to the other side, then added solder to the pads on the bottom side of the circuit board as well, just below the pads on the top. After reinstalling the decoder, I tested it again and got much better results.

On the second model, I had good contact, but the motor wouldn't move. After taking the decoder off the frame, I saw that the upper motor contact was touching the frame. Digitrax has a feature on its newer decoders that prevents power from being sent to the motor if it isn't isolated from the frame. I moved the motor contact away from the frame and slipped a bit of Kapton tape between the contact and frame to be sure of isolating the circuits. I then reinstalled the decoder. Success!

Still, the models didn't start moving until speed step 4 of 28, so I went back to the programming track and did a

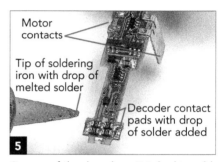

On one of the decoders, Eric had to add a drop of solder to thicken the contact pads and improve electrical contact between the decoder and frame.

little more adjustment. Using the NCE Power Cab DCC system we have connected to our test track, I first set the controller at speed step 1. Then I went into the menu for programming on the main and chose motor starting voltage (Configuration Variable 2). The values can be anything from 0 to 255.

Once I was in programming mode with the first locomotive, I started by entering 10, which got a slight bump from the motor, but no movement. Cycling through the programming options to bring me back to CV2, I kept adding a higher number until I just got the locomotive to move. For the first engine, that value was 40. The second, which ran better on DC power to begin with, only required a value of 30 to get it moving.

Although it took a little more than just dropping in the decoders, the whole process was pretty painless. Give it a try and in an evening you'll have another locomotive or two added to your DCC roster.

Programming decoders

To enjoy the full benefits of decoders, some programming is necessary. The amount of tweaking you do to the configuration variables (CVs) is a matter of personal preference, but at the very least you'll want to give the decoder a unique address. Most modelers prefer using the locomotive's road number (or part of it) for the decoder's address, as it's easy to remember.

Depending on your decoder's features, you can further enhance a locomotive's realism by adjusting the speed, momentum, and lighting effects. If you plan on running multi-engine consists, you can speed match locomotives, as explained on pages 52-53. This is especially useful if you're running locomotives from different manufacturers.

Other topics we'll cover in Chapter 4 include basic decoder programming, consisting, motor performance, and function mapping. We'll also take an in-depth look at CV29, a special configuration variable that activates several basic features.

Basic decoder programming

Running multiple locomotives with decoders on the same layout requires some basic programming. At the very least, each Digital Command Control (DCC) decoder must have a unique address.

The decoder's address is contained in a configuration variable (CV). CVs are stored in non-volatile memory. This means when the power goes off, the CVs retain their value. For example, CV1 contains the value of the primary address of the decoder.

Programming CVs

There are two basic ways to program CVs. The first is on a programming track, also called service mode. Many DCC systems have two sets of track terminals on them. One set goes to your layout to run your trains. The other is for a programming track. A DCC system uses one or the other depending on whether you're programming or running trains. The programming track output doesn't provide enough current to run trains.

A programming track should be a section of track that's electrically iso-

Before you enjoy running multiple locomotives on the same layout with DCC, you need to do some basic decoder programming. *Jim Forbes photos*

lated from the rest of your layout. Mine is at my workbench. Make sure there's only one engine on the track at a time when you're programming. If there are multiple engines on the track, they'll all be programmed to the same address.

Some modelers have a spur on their layout that serves as both a programming track and an active track. The track is isolated by cutting gaps in both rails or by using insulated rail joiners.

A double-pole double-throw (DPDT) switch is used to select the main line or programming track. Be aware that if a locomotive or lighted passenger car crosses the gaps while programming, you could end up accidentally programming all the locomotives on your layout.

An advantage to using a track on your layout is you don't have to lift the locomotive off the layout and set it on the programming track.

The NCE Power Cab, Bachmann EZ-Command, and older Digitrax systems use the same terminals for both

The back of Model Rectifier Corp.'s Prodigy Advance command station features screw terminals for the main and programming tracks.

The NCE Power Cab uses the same terminals for mainline and programming tracks. With this system, the entire main line is the programming track.

mainline and programming tracks. Any locomotive on the main will be programmed when in programming mode. To prevent this, a separate programming track can be set up with connections directly to command station terminals and a switch that you must turn off to separate the main from command station terminals. NCE sells the Auto-SW that does this automatically.

Not only can decoder CVs be written on the programming track, but they can also be read. Some DCC systems read back the value of a CV before it's programmed. To do this, the DCC system continually "asks" the decoder if the CV is a particular value. If it isn't, nothing happens and the DCC system asks if it's a different value.

When it finally finds the right value, the decoder "acknowledges" by pulsing the motor briefly. The DCC system detects the increased current and knows it guessed the right value. Depending on the actual value of the CV, it might take a few moments to guess the right value.

This method worked well until sound decoders were added to locomotives. Some sound decoders draw more current than programming tracks were originally designed for. Digital Command Control systems could no longer detect an "acknowledge."

In addition, some decoders draw so much current that the programming track can't supply enough to program them. This varies between DCC systems and decoders. Both SoundTraxx and DCC Specialties make programming track boosters that allow sound decoders to be programmed.

Don't confuse programming boost-

ers with power boosters used to provide power to the main. Programming boosters don't have to be removed when programming non-sound decoders.

Dirty wheels and track, as well as miswired decoders, might cause difficulties in programming or reading back CVs. In most locomotive decoders, the motor must be wired for the acknowledge to occur. One of the best methods to determine if you have installed a decoder correctly is to read back a CV on the programming track.

The limited current available on the programming track might protect a miswired decoder from damage. If you can read back a CV, you know that at least the track power and motor connections are wired correctly.

There are different methods for controlling programming. CVP's Easy DCC and Digitrax's Zephyr use buttons and displays on the command station. Larger Digitrax systems, Model Rectifier Corp., Lenz, and NCE use throttles.

Many systems support computer interfacing, which enables you to use computer software to program a decoder. This is often the easiest way to program CVs. Programs like the free Decoder Pro software available at jmri. sourceforge.net/help/en/html/apps/ DecoderPro/ have menus and screens that guide you through the process.

There are also stand-alone programmers from companies like QSI Solutions, Digitrax, and ESU (LokSound). These are connected to a computer and are primarily used for downloading new sounds and firmware

updates into their decoders. They also include software for programming CVs and can be used with any manufacturer's decoders. Never connect these programmers to your DCC system.

Ops-mode programming

Most modern decoders and DCC systems allow programming on the main, also known as operations-mode programming. Just about everything that can be adjusted on a programming track can be done on the main. Some decoders don't allow you to program the address on the main.

But there are several advantages to operations-mode programming. First, you can tweak CV settings while on the main. This gives you instant feedback when speed matching locomotives or other motor performance CVs. There is also enough current available to program sound decoders.

Unlike service-mode programming, operations mode only programs the addressed locomotive. However, both the decoder and the DCC system must support ops-mode programming for this to work.

One drawback to operations-mode programming is most systems can't read back the values in CVs.

Programming locomotive decoders lets you enjoy the many benefits of DCC, including prototypical lighting, momentum effects, and realistic speed, among other features. Yes, programming decoders requires practice and some experimentation, but once you get the hang of it, you'll have even more fun running trains with DCC.

Configuration variable (CV) basics

Mobile decoders used in locomotives and stationary decoders used to operate accessories can be customized using configuration variables (CVs). Think of a CV like a file folder with a piece of paper in it. With your DCC system, you can write a number on that piece of paper and put it back in the folder. The decoder can look at the number in the folder and act upon its value. Since there are many CVs, there are many different file folders in a single decoder.

Types of CVs
Configuration variables range from the very simple (decoder address) to more complex (back-electromotive-force control). The CVs control a variety of features, from lighting effects to what style of horn is played by a sound decoder.

Not all makers' decoders have the same CVs, and even those that do often don't work in the same way. There are, however, several essential CVs designated by the National Model Railroad Association (NMRA) to operate the same way in all decoders.

One of those is CV1. This is the primary address, sometimes called the two-digit or short address. When the DCC system instructs a decoder what to do, it first sends an address through the rails so a specific decoder knows to listen for commands. The values for CV1 can be 0 to 127, but not all systems use the entire range. In some decoders, a value of 0 for CV1 takes

the decoder out of DCC. Other DCC systems don't use addresses between 100-127, making it truly a two-digit address.

I find the range of 1-127 too limiting for my decoder addresses, so I make use of CVs 17 and 18, which are the extended address CVs, sometimes called the four-digit or long address. This lets me use the locomotive's three- or four-digit road number for the decoder address. Configuration variables 17 and 18 combine to create any number between 1 and 10,239, though many DCC systems limit that range. Some systems treat any address below 100 as a primary address, while others will not support addresses above 9,999. A few DCC systems won't recognize extended addresses at all.

Knowing how CVs 17 and 18 work is important because it's possible to program a locomotive on one layout and move it to another model railroad that has different decoder restrictions and not be able to use it.

For example, you may program the extended address to 35 with one DCC system and then try to operate it on another layout where that isn't a valid four-digit address. When you select that locomotive with a throttle, it will recognize a two-digit address as a locomotive with CV1 programmed to 35 instead of CV17 and CV18 programmed to 35, and you won't be able to operate it. In this case, CV29 must be programmed to tell the decoder to use the extended address instead of the primary address.

Now that sounds complicated, doesn't it? Sometimes it is. Combining CV17 and CV18 to create a number for an address isn't always an easy task. Thankfully, most DCC systems take care of the math for you. Often, the fact that you're programming these

Bit number	Bit 0	Bit 1	Bit 2	Bit 3	Bit 4	Bit 5	Bit 6	Bit 7
Value	1	2	4	8	16	32	64	128
Purpose	Direction	Obsolete	Power conversion	Bi-directional communication	Speed table	Extended addressing	Reserved	Accessory decoder

Configuration variable 29 controls more than simply what address to use for a decoder. This table shows the different bit numbers, values, and purposes.

CVs is completely transparent to the user. All you need to know is that you want to program the four-digit address.

Configuration variable 29 is a unique CV because it controls many important features. Some DCC systems configure CV29 automatically, but others do not. To program CV29 yourself, you must learn a little bit of how a computer works.

Computers use numbers in the form of bytes (pronounced "bites"). Each byte is made up of 8 bits, and each bit can be either a "1" or a "0".

Each CV is one byte of information, so there are 8 bits numbered 0-7 (computer engineers prefer counting things starting with zero). The bits of information in CV29 enable or disable features. To get the number to program into a CV, add up the value of each bit, as in the chart above.

Bit functions

What does each bit do? Bit 0 controls whether the locomotive moves forward or back when the throttle is set to forward. A zero in bit 0 means forward, and a one in bit 0 means reverse. This is useful with a wired decoder where, during installation, the gray and orange wires to the motor are accidentally reversed. It's also helpful with a drop-in decoder when you want the locomotive to run long hood forward.

Bit 1 is basically a holdover from the early days of DCC using 14 speed steps. It's largely ignored by modern decoders.

Bit 2 controls whether the locomotive converts to DC or another command control system in the absence of a DCC signal.

Bit 3 enables bi-directional communication. Not all decoders or DCC systems support this.

Bit 4 enables a speed table. Speed tables are helpful when you're speed matching different locomotives. (See more on speed matching on pages 52-53).

Bit 5 enables CV17 and 18 to be used for addressing the locomotive.

Bits 6 and 7 aren't used on most locomotive decoders.

How does this all work? If you want your locomotive to travel in reverse with the throttle set to forward and to enable extended addressing, you'd add the values for bits 0 and 5 and program that value into CV29 (1 + 32 = 33.)

Many other CVs are divided into separate bits like this as well. Each bit of the CV controls a feature. Added up, the bit values give the final value to program into that CV. Many CVs just use the total value, such as CV2, the start voltage. The higher the CV value, the more voltage is applied to the motor at speed step 1 set by the throttle.

Changing CVs

There are a few ways to change CVs. Most DCC systems have terminals on the command station for a programming track. These are connected to a piece of track isolated from the rest of the layout. Mine is on my workbench, but you could use a siding as long as it's electrically isolated from the rest of the layout.

A locomotive on a programming track can have its CVs changed in service mode programming. Using the DCC throttle or a control panel, the CV can be modified or read back. Only one locomotive can be on the programming track at a time. Some sound decoders draw more current than some programming tracks can supply. SoundTraxx and DCC Specialties sell programming boosters to overcome that problem.

Certain decoders and DCC systems will also take advantage of operations-mode programming, or programming on the main. This uses any track on your layout to program CVs. Any number of locomotives can be on the track at the same time.

Reading back CVs on the screen of your throttle is useful when you're experimenting with CV values like speed matching, ditch light flashing rate, or sound volume. However, CVs can't be read back in operations mode.

If programming CVs seems complicated, don't worry. Other than the locomotive address, you don't have to program any CVs. However, there are several ways to figure out how to program CVs. Many decoder manuals contain step-by-step instructions. Some DCC systems are very intuitive and walk you through the steps in plain English. In my opinion, the coolest method for programming CVs is with a computer.

There are several ways to connect your computer to your decoder. The first is through your DCC system. Many DCC systems have computer interfaces available. Software, such as the free DecoderPro (jmri.sourceforge.net), allows you to select decoder features with the click of a mouse. Model Rectifier Corp. also has decoder programming software (www.modelrec.com).

You can also connect your computer to your decoder through programming boxes such as Digitrax's PS3, QSISolutions' Quantum Programmer, and ESU's LokSound Programmer. Originally intended for programming sound decoders, they also allow you to program other CVs. Each is a small box that connects to either the USB or serial port of your computer and to your programming track. Do not connect these boxes to your DCC system.

Configuration variables may sound intimidating, but with a little patience and the aid of your DCC system or computer, you can get the most out of your decoder.

How to speed match locomotives

Speed matching is important if you want two or more diesel locomotives to run well in a multiple-unit consist. There are a couple of ways to do this by programming decoder configuration variables. *Bill Zuback*

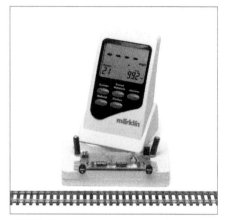

Märklin is one of several manufacturers that produce speedometers that can be used in multiple scales. *Jim Forbes*

In the days before DCC, it was common to remotor or regear locomotives so they'd run well together. Getting the operating characteristics of all locomotives as close as possible was desirable for operating well in a multiple-unit diesel consist or double-heading steam locomotives. If the locomotives didn't operate similarly, the faster locomotive would pull or push the slower one around the layout, drastically reducing the number of cars that could be pulled and leading to derailments and other operational problems.

Thanks to DCC, we can now fine-tune motor operation so locomotives produced by different manufacturers can run together smoothly.

Speedometer

If you have more than a couple of locomotives to speed match, I recommend using a speedometer to record speed. I use the Trainspeed speedometer from TDP & Associates, but other speedometers, such as the one from Märklin pictured above, work just as well. In addition, the creators of the decoder programming tool Decoder Pro have free software for making a speedom-

eter out of DCC block detectors used for signaling and other applications. It can be found at jmri.sourceforge.net. Decoder Pro is also useful for programming configuration variables (CVs) to create speed curves and speed tables.

For the purpose of speed matching locomotives, accuracy isn't as important as consistency. In other words, it's not important if your speedometer reads 35 scale miles per hour when the locomotive is actually running 45 scale mph, as long as every time a locomotive runs at a given speed the speedometer shows the same reading.

Speed curves

There are two ways to match locomotive speeds. Perhaps the easiest to implement is using CV2, CV5, and CV6. These three CVs work together to create a speed curve.

Before starting, make sure your track and locomotive wheels are clean. You'll also need a throttle that has a readout of the throttle position. (Some throttles don't indicate the speed step command they're sending to the locomotive.)

It's almost essential to use operations-mode programming, also called

programming on the main. Moving a locomotive between the programming track and the main line is far too tedious for the amount of adjustment speed matching requires. I have my speedometer sensors permanently positioned on the main line of my layout. The readout is mounted in the fascia. There should also be enough room to get the locomotive up to full speed and, just as importantly, enough room for it to stop.

Configuration variable 2 (Vstart) allows you to adjust the motor voltage in speed step one. Its valid range is from 0-255. The higher the number, the higher percentage of track voltage is applied to the motor. I adjust CV2 so my locomotives start moving at about 4 scale mph. You might have to adjust other motor characteristics like back-electro-motive-force control (back-EMF), torque compensation, or "dither" to get the locomotive to move at speed step one. Since every decoder is different in that aspect, you'll need to consult the appropriate decoder manual. CVs 5 and 6 are optional, and not all decoders have these CVs.

Configuration variable 5 is the Vhigh adjustment. It adjusts the motor

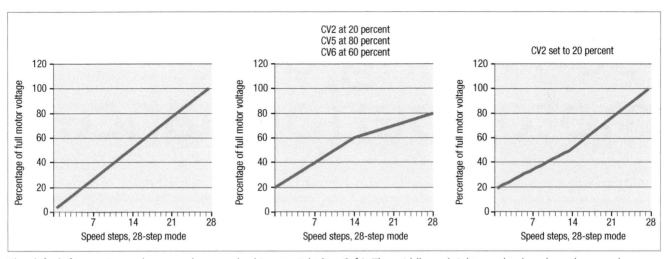

The default for most speed curves when graphed is a straight line (left). The middle and right graphs show how the speed curve looks when configuration variables 2, 5, and 6 have been adjusted.

voltage at full throttle. This can be either speed step 28 or speed step 128, depending on the speed mode used. Adjust this CV before adjusting CV6.

Configuration variable 6 is Vmid. It adjusts the motor voltage at speed step 14 or 64, depending on which speed mode is used. I set my locomotives to run at about 30 scale mph at mid-throttle.

You might be wondering how to find the correct number to program CV5 and CV6 to get the desired results. It's possible, and sometimes quicker, to do this by trial and error. You might also consider using a pencil and paper (or calculator) and doing a little math.

The trial-and-error method is simply running the locomotive, checking its speed at the throttle position you're trying to adjust, and guessing a number to program into the CV. Repeat this process and fine tune it until you find the correct number.

By doing a little math, it's possible to make better guesses. The first step is to find the default for CV5 and CV6. Run the locomotive at full throttle and record the speed. Multiply the default CV value (or the value you last set it to) by your desired speed (70 scale mph for me) and divide that number by the measured speed. That should give you a number close to the correct value for CV5.

For example, say the default value for CV5 is 255, and your locomotive runs a scale 100 mph at speed step 28

in 28-speed-step mode. If you want to set it to 70 scale mph, multiply 255 by 70, and divide the result (17,850) by 100 (178.5). You can program CV5 to either 178 or 179.

For CV6, set the throttle at mid-speed (speed step 14 or 64) and measure the locomotive's speed. Repeat the calculation but substitute the default value for CV6 (or the value you last set it to). These numbers should be close to the correct value, but you can always use trial and error from this point to fine tune the value.

What happens at the other throttle positions depends on the decoder. Some brands draw a straight line between speed step 1 and mid-throttle (14/64), and another between mid-throttle and full throttle (28/128). Other manufacturers use some sort of curve.

The charts above show how speed curves work. The factory default for many decoders divide the voltage to the motor evenly between steps. When this is graphed, the speed curve is a straight line.

The middle graph shows how the speed curve changes when CV2 is set to 51, increasing the starting voltage to 20 percent.

The right-hand graph shows how the speed curve from the middle graph changed when CV6 is set to 153 (60 percent) and CV5 to 204 (80 percent). Setting CV5 to 80 percent limits how fast the locomotive can go at step 28, or full throttle.

Speed tables

With a decoder that doesn't have CV5 and CV6, it might be necessary to program a speed table by using CVs 67-94. Each of these CVs controls a single speed step in the 28-speed step mode. If you're using 128 speed steps, the CVs control about every 4½ speed steps.

Some, but not all, decoders have built-in speed tables or allow you to make your own. If you're going to match different manufacturers' decoders, you'll probably have to make your own. Decide what speed you want each step to be and, just as with Vhigh and Vmid, calculate the value for full throttle and mid-throttle. Fill in the values for the rest of the steps by dividing the difference in CV values by the number of intermediate steps between step 1 and step 14, and then again between step 14 and step 28.

To activate the speed table, you must enable it using CV29. The actual value you program into CV29 varies with the options you select. One of the best charts I've seen for determining the value of CV29 is on page 18 of the SoundTraxx LC series owner's manual (found online at www.soundtraxx.com/manuals/lc_manual.pdf).

Once you think you have your locomotives speed matched, test them by placing them in a consist but separating them by a foot or so. Run them at various throttle settings to see if they move at approximately the same speed. No matter how hard you try, they won't be exact, but close is good enough.

Consisting and motor performance

Just like real railroads, model railroaders often run multiple locomotives on the same train. Using DCC, there are a number of ways to run two or more locomotives in the same consist.

Each locomotive has a DCC decoder to convert the digital signal in the rails to a voltage that controls the motor. In order to run each locomotive independently, a decoder has a unique address programmed through the use of a configuration variable (CV).

There are two types of addresses: short (CV1) and long (CVs 17 and 18 together). The short address is often called the two-digit address, and the long address is referred to as the four-digit. A portion of CV29 controls which is the active address. The seemingly complicated task of programming addresses is often made easier through the use of a menu-driven operation, which is available in some DCC command stations, as well as through computer programs, such as Decoder Pro (jmri.sourceforge.net) and Model Rectifier's Prodigy DCC Computer Interface.

Consisting

The simplest way to run multiple locomotives together with one throttle is to program each decoder to the same address. The DCC throttle sends one command to one address through the rails, and all of the decoders will respond. To operate locomotives in opposite directions, the decoders' motor leads must be wired opposite from each other, or you can use CV29 to reprogram the direction bit. If CV29 is an even number, the locomotive will run forward. If the number is odd, the engine will run in reverse.

This method works well with locomotives that are permanently coupled together. In the early days of diesel road locomotives, it wasn't uncommon to have a set of F units connected with drawbars. Railroads soon discovered that one of the advantages of diesel locomotives was to break consists apart if one of the locomotives wasn't operating properly or if more or less power is needed. If you're modeling a period after the late 1940s, you'll probably want to mix and match your locomotives. Reprogramming locomotive addresses every time you break and make a consist is cumbersome using the single-address approach.

Another way to program multiple units is with universal consisting. This is accomplished through your DCC system command station. Each DCC system sets up universal consisting a little differently, and some don't support it.

After setup, the command station receives a single command from a throttle. The station then sends out a separate message to each locomotive in the consist.

Though no programming is done to the decoders and each decoder retains its original address, universal consisting does have some drawbacks. On layouts with many universal consists, several commands must be sent, which can affect the performance of your DCC system. Universal consisting won't work if you operate on both your home layout and a club layout and want to maintain consists between the two, unless you've programmed both DCC systems with the same universal consist.

A third way of consisting with DCC is called advanced consisting. Some decoders have a special configuration variable, CV19, that contains a short (two-digit) address and a direction bit. If the address portion of CV19 is non-zero, the decoder responds to the address programmed into CV19 instead of its normal active address. Not all decoders have CV19, so it's not as "universal" as universal consisting, but it has some advantages.

Unlike universal consisting, advanced consisting is portable. A set of locomotives can be moved from layout to layout and remain consisted. However, this approach requires that you remember the consist address, most likely not one of the locomotive road numbers. Universal consisting can be a problem if the locomotives in the consist are removed from the layout and not replaced facing in the correct directions.

If you have a problem with locomotives that were part of an advanced consist, create a new advanced consist using the same engines and then delete that consist. This will reprogram all the decoders' consist addresses (CV19) to zero.

With some DCC systems the consist address is programmed into the decoders and the DCC command station. This isn't a requirement, but it can be a convenience. The command station not only assigns the next available two-digit consist address to the decoders, but it uses each end of the consists' primary address as a consist alias. The end that is selected is considered the forward direction.

Matching speeds

Operating multiple units together can cause some mechanical problems. If the locomotives operate at drastically different speeds at the same throttle position, bucking and hunting can occur, especially when going up or down a grade. The best way to solve this problem is to speed match your locomotives. This involves setting a number of motor performance CVs, which can get pretty involved. You can

With DCC consisting and motor control features, this Atlas Dash 8-40B and Athearn SD40-2 run well together. Mike gives three examples of how to consist locomotives. *Bill Zuback*

learn more details about speed matching on pages 52-53.

The goal of speed matching is to establish a speed for each throttle position and try to set all your locomotives to it. I've found this easiest to achieve with a model railroad speedometer, available from Bachrus, TDP & Associates, and Märklin, among others.

Having a DCC system and decoders that allow for operations-mode programming (also called programming on the main) makes it easier to adjust motor performance CVs. In fact, I couldn't imagine doing this without it.

Configuration variables 2, 5, and 6 are perhaps the easiest speed matching CVs to use. These CVs are present in most National Model Railroad Association-compliant decoders.

Configuration variable 2 is the start voltage. By increasing or decreasing this CV's value, it's possible to set your locomotive to start moving at throttle position 1. This gets complicated in decoders with back-electromotive-force control or other low-speed motor control. The CVs for those adjustments vary between manufacturers and are covered in each decoder's manual. Some decoders don't use CV1 when back-EMF is enabled.

Configuration variable 5 is the high voltage control. By adjusting this CV, you can control the top speed of the decoder when the throttle is set at its maximum value (28 for 28 speed steps or 128 for 128 speed steps). Configuration variable 6 is the mid-range. Configuration variables 2, 5, and

6 create a curve (not to be confused with a speed curve) that controls how fast the locomotive runs at each throttle position.

When using decoders from different manufacturers in locomotives from different companies, you may find that a three-point curve isn't adequate. Many DCC decoders also have speed curves or speed tables. This allows you to set a locomotive speed for every throttle speed step. I find this is the best way to speed match locomotives. Again, how these are implemented varies between decoder brands.

Running multiple locomotives from one throttle isn't as hard as it sounds. By using one of the speed matching techniques described here, your consist will look great and run smoothly.

Exploring momentum effects

Commuter trains, like this one at Lombard, Ill., have to accelerate and decelerate rapidly for frequent station stops. Mike explains using momentum effects in DCC decoders to duplicate prototype performance.

Imagine that you're the engineer of a Metra commuter train in Chicago. You're running a 3,000-horsepower locomotive with four commuter coaches behind you, as shown in the photo above. In order to keep the time-table schedule, you must quickly accelerate from every station, and quickly decelerate for the next stop. With such a light train, quick starts and stops are possible.

Now imagine you're in charge of the Burlington Northern coal train on the opposite page. This 10,000-ton train handles quite differently. Even with five locomotives, those fast starts and stops are no longer possible. That's because the trains have different momentum.

Momentum is the product of velocity and mass. In other words, the heavier the train and the faster it's going, the more momentum it has and the harder it is to change speeds quickly.

Modeling momentum

In model railroading, there's not much difference between the way a commuter train and coal train handle. However, with DCC you can simulate momen-tum by adjusting certain configuration variables (CVs) in motor decoders.

The primary momentum CVs are CV3 and CV4. Configuration variable 3 adjusts the acceleration and CV4 adjusts the deceleration in most decod-ers. The higher the value of the CV, the longer it takes for the decoder to respond to a change in a speed-step command.

National Model Railroad Association Recommended Practice 9.2.2 has an equation for calculating momentum: The value of the CV x .896/the number of speed steps.

For example, if the value of CV3 is 47 and the decoder is set up for 28 speed steps, take 47 x 0.896/28. It would take a locomotive 1.5 seconds to respond to a change of a single speed step. To go from a stop to full speed, take 1.5 x 28. It would take a locomotive 42 seconds to reach maximum speed.

Since this equation is only an NMRA recommended practice and not a standard, decoder manufacturers are free to create any formula they like. That's unfortunate if you use decoders from different companies and try to consist locomotives.

However, it's possible to calculate the value of CV3 for each decoder. The same holds true for CV4. For example, Digitrax decoders allow values between 0 and 32 for CV3 and CV4. A value of zero means no momentum. Increasing the value by one increases the delay by 100 milliseconds. The most delay that can be programmed per speed step is 3.2 seconds. To get 1.5 seconds per step as in the previous example above, you'd have to program CV3 to 15.

Momentum on the go

NCE's PowerCab (below) and ProCab throttles program CVs 3 and 4 automatically. Once a locomotive or consist is selected, you may push the momentum button and enter a number from 0 to 9. That number is multiplied by eight and entered into CV3 of every unit in the consist. Half that value is entered into CV4, meaning deceleration has less momentum.

Some decoders use CV23 and CV24. These CVs can fine tune momentum by adding or subtracting a little from the values held in CV3 and CV4. The NMRA does have a uniform specification for these CVs, meaning that all manufacturers are supposed to follow the same convention. Values of 128 and above add delay to the value programmed in CV3

The NCE Power Cab throttle has a dedicated momentum button.

Five 3,000-hp locomotives are in charge of this 10,000-ton coal train near Crawford, Neb. Unlike the commuter train on the opposite page, fast starts and stops aren't possible with a long, heavy coal train like this. *Dan Poitras*

and CV4, while values below subtract delay.

SoundTraxx's Tsunami decoders have a feature that lets you adjust the braking momentum using your throttle's F11 function button. Placing a value between 1 and 128 in CV61 makes your train stop more slowly than it would normally by adding to the value in CV4 when you press F11. A value of 129 to 255 in CV61 allows F11 to temporarily subtract from the value of CV4, bringing the train to a stop more quickly.

Train Control Systems has an interesting twist on programming momentum. It recognizes that you may not want the same response at every throttle position. Some of its decoders use additional CVs that allow you to program a momentum curve similar to a speed curve. Configuration variables 3 and 4 still set the momentum rate closest to stop, but other CVs set the speed step in which the momentum changes. The firm's decoders have three different momentum rates for acceleration and deceleration.

For acceleration, CV129 controls the second starting point, and CV130 controls the second rate. Configuration variable 131 controls the third starting point, and CV132 controls the third rate.

For deceleration, CV125 controls the second starting point, CV126 controls the second rate, and CV127 sets the third starting point and CV128 controls the third. A chart of this can be found on the TCS website, www.tcsdcc.com/Customer_Content/Technical_Info/Tech_Manuals/Additional.pdf.

Since each manufacturer has its own way of calculating momentum, decoders may end up with different acceleration and deceleration rates. The amount of momentum you program into a locomotive may vary depending on its purpose (passenger or freight) and the size of your model railroad.

Adding momentum to locomotives will add realism to your operating session. No longer will your operators be able to stop on a dime at a signal or station. They'll have to plan their moves well ahead, just like a real engineer.

Advanced headlight programming

Soo Line GP9 no. 552 has its headlights on bright, appropriate for trains occupying the main line. The Geep's sister unit, no. 554, has its headlights dimmed, which is correct for a meet per Rule 17.

The operation of DCC decoders can be modified with configuration variables (CVs). What can be programmed depends on the decoder, but most offer motor control and lighting effects, and some for sound. Each manufacturer's decoders are different, so what applies to one decoder may not apply to another. However, one thing all decoders have in common is how a CV's value is calculated.

Configuration variables are 8 bits long. A bit is a single value, either 0 or 1. Digital engineers begin counting with 0 so the first bit (usually shown at the right of the number) is called bit 0, which has a weight of 1. If bit 0 is set to 1 and all the other bits are at a 0, then the value of the entire CV is 1.

The next bit, 1, has a weight of 2. If bit 1 is set to 1 and all other bits are set to 0, then the value of the entire CV is 2. If bit 0 and bit 1 are both set to 1, add the bit weights (bit 0 = 1 and bit 1 = 2) to get a value of 3. Each bit weight is twice the previous bit's weight, so bit 7's weight is 128. By adding the weights of only the bits that are set to 1, any number between 0 and 255 can be obtained.

Many DCC decoder manuals include CV charts. In some CVs, like CV29 found in all decoders, each bit represents a different feature. By choosing which features are desired and setting the corresponding bit to 1, the value that needs to be programmed into the CV can be determined by adding the bit weights of all the selected features.

As an example, we'll take a look at the QS Industries (QSI) Quantum sound decoder found in many brands of locomotives, including my HO scale Proto 2000 GP9 shown in the photo.

Out of the box, the GP9 has several automatic lighting features. QSI decoders have three directions: forward, reverse, and neutral. Different lighting effects can be programmed to occur when the locomotive is moving forward, transitioning from forward to neutral, and transitioning from reverse to neutral.

The headlight is factory programmed to be dim in neutral only.

It becomes bright at speed step 1 and above. Like many decoders, the lighting is directional. If you select F0 on the DCC throttle, then only the front headlight is lit when the locomotive is moving forward and only the rear headlight is lit when the locomotive is moving in reverse. If you deselect F0, the headlights are off.

My model railroad is set in 1963 and abides by the Consolidated Code of Operating Rules of 1959. Rule 17 says, among many other things, that the headlight of a train must be on bright while occupying the main track. This applies if the locomotive is moving or not. This is crucial at a meet where the train that is supposed to take the siding can't clear the main track. The bright headlight serves as a warning to the opposing train.

Rule 17 also states that a train's headlight must be dimmed when approaching another train. Therefore, the headlight on my model must be dimmable while the locomotive is moving. Finally, Rule 18 states that yard engines will display a headlight to the front and rear at the same time. In order to make my QSI-equipped locomotives match the rest of the fleet and conform to Rules 17 and 18, I had to reprogram its CVs.

QSI decoders

Original equipment manufacturer QSI Quantum decoders are supported by QSI Solutions. The firm offers a chip upgrade for older QSI decoders to update them to version R7. From there, you can use the Quantum Programmer and a personal computer to update the chips. The programming described below is for version R7 decoders and newer.

The programming can be done with any DCC system that supports a pro-

Example of a configuration variable								
Feature	H	G	F	E	D	C	B	A
Bit number	7	6	5	4	3	2	1	0
Weight	128	64	32	16	8	4	2	1
Value	0	1	0	0	0	1	1	0
If you want features B, C, and G active, set the appropriate bits and add their weights.								
Feature B = 2, feature C = 4, feature G = 64. 2 + 4 + 64 = 70.								
Program the value 70 into the appropriate CV.								

gramming track. Some DCC systems might also require a programming track booster. These are available from DCC Specialties and SoundTraxx.

I wanted the front headlight to be controlled by F0 regardless of direction and dimmed by F4. Likewise, I wanted the rear headlight to be controlled by F3 and dimmed by F5.

The Quantum decoder is one of the most flexible decoders I've encountered. However, with flexibility comes complexity. There are literally hundreds of CVs, and the current DCC Reference Manual (found at www.qsisolutions. com) is 383 pages long. That sounds intimidating, but like many other aspects of DCC, you can learn as you go.

In order to get that many CVs, QSI uses indirect addressing, or paging. This means there is one or more index CVs. In QSI's case, the primary index is CV49.

One of the CVs I used to get the realistic lighting I wanted was CV55. There are several CV55s, and each one controls a different lighting effect. The front and rear headlights are CV55.70 and CV55.73, respectively. Digital Command Control systems can only program one CV55, however. They don't know anything beyond the decimal point. That's where CV49 comes in. Which CV55 is programmed by the DCC system depends on the value programmed into CV49. To program CV55.70, I first programmed CV49 to 70. Then whatever value is programmed into CV55 will go into CV55.70.

QSI takes this one step further with a secondary index controlled by CV50. This extends the CV number to one more decimal point. In reality it's not just CV55.70 but CV55.70.0.

Configuration variable 55 is expressed as CV55.PI.SI, where PI is the primary index (CV49) and SI is the secondary index (CV50). Just like CV49, CV50 must be programmed with the secondary index prior to programming CV55. To program value CV55.70.12, first write 70 to CV49, then 12 to CV50, and then the desired value to CV55. It doesn't matter which index (CV49 or CV50) is written to first as long as they are both programmed before CV55.

Programming lighting

Now that you have some background of primary and secondary indexes, follow along as I take you through the steps I used to program my GP9 lighting to follow Rules 17 and 18. I highly recommend referring to QSI's Quantum DCC Reference Manual as you go through these steps.

First, I programmed the front headlight. The DCC Reference Manual indicates that CV55.70.0 controls the headlight initial state when powered up.

The default value is 1 (bit 0 = 1), which means that feature 70 is active. A chart on page 126 of revision 5.0.2 of the manual shows that feature 70 is the automatic headlight that I wanted to eliminate in favor of manual control. I didn't want the headlight to be on initially (bit 1) or dim (bit 2), so I changed the value of CV55.70.0 from a 1 to a 0 (no bits set). To do this, I first programmed the primary index (CV49) to 70 and the secondary index (CV50) to 0. Then I programmed CV55 to 0.

I also had to program CV55.136.0 from the default value of 255 (all features on) to 0 (all features off). I reprogrammed CV49 to 136 before programming CV55. Since I'd just programmed CV55.70.0, CV50 was

already at 0 and I didn't need to reprogram it. This can get very confusing, so I always program both CV49 and CV50 each time I program a CV.

Next, I programmed the front headlight to turn on and off with function 0 on my throttles regardless of direction. Configuration variable 53 controls the function outputs and is outlined in sections 5.6 and 5.6.1 of the manual. Scanning the chart, I found feature 71 (headlight explicitly on) is what I wanted for CV53, specifically CV53.1.0 "Feature Assigned to Output 1 in FWD/REV." To do that, I needed to program CV49 to 1, CV50 to 0, and CV53 to 71.

The rest of the front headlight programming was similar. I programmed CV53.1.1 to 71. To get the headlight to dim with F4, I programmed CV53.6.0 to 72 and CV53.6.1 to 72.

The values to program the rear headlight are CV55.73.0 = 0, CV55.136.0 = 0 (already done for the front headlight), CV53.5.0 = 74, and CV53.5.1 = 74. To make the rear headlight dim with F5, I programmed CV53.7.0 to 75 and CV53.7.1 to 75. However, these CVs wouldn't program with the revision of firmware in my decoder.

To adjust the brightness of the front headlight when dimmed, program CV55.70.10 to any number from 1 to 255. The higher the number, the brighter the light. I programmed the CV to 127. The Quantum Programmer used for updating the firmware of QSI Quantum decoders can also be used with its free Quantum CV Manager software. With that software, the primary (CV49) and secondary (CV50) indexes are automatically managed.

The Quantum Programmer also works as a mini DCC command station so you can test your programming without connecting to your DCC system.

This is just an example of what can be done with advanced CVs. Although this can be complicated, don't be scared off. Part of the fun is trying different things. When experimenting, write down the default or previous values of the CVs you are changing so that you can restore those values if needed.

Understanding function mapping

Adjusting the controls for lights, sounds, and other effects on your Digital Command Control-equipped locomotives is possible with function mapping. *Jim Forbes*

Besides controlling the speed and direction of a locomotive, DCC throttles are also capable of controlling lights, sounds, and other effects. This is done with function buttons. Pressing a function button turns on a particular locomotive feature.

The default setting for most decoders is that function button 0 (F0) controls the front headlight when the locomotive is moving forward and the rear headlight when the engine is in reverse. Likewise, F1 usually controls the bell in a sound decoder, or whatever is attached to the green wire in a wired non-sound decoder. Function button 2 (F2) controls the whistle/horn, or effect attached to the violet wire.

I prefer that the headlight not automatically switch directions with the locomotive. To change this feature, I "map" the functions so that different buttons control different outputs. This requires reprogramming configuration variables (CVs). Configuration variables are stored in a decoder and affect the way a locomotive responds when receiving a command from a DCC system.

The National Model Railroad Association (NMRA) recommends that CVs 33-46 be used for this purpose. This is just a recommendation, so not all DCC decoders use these CVs. Even if they do, they may not always be used in the same manner.

Chart **1** shows the NMRA recommendation for CVs 33 through 46. The "D" is the default setting. This indicates that when traveling forward, F0 controls decoder output 1, the white wire on a wired decoder, usually connected to the forward headlight.

Reprogramming CV33 will allow F0 to control other decoder functions. The tan boxes are function outputs that can't be controlled by a specific function button.

CVs and functions

A CV is an eight-bit digital number, so only eight function outputs can be assigned to a particular function button. Chart **2** at right shows a method that many decoders use to program the CVs.

In this case, CV33's default value is 1, which means F0 (forward) controls output 1 (the white wire). To change which function output is controlled by F0 (forward), choose the output to be controlled and program the number in that column to the CV corresponding to the function button you want to use.

For example, on my decoders, I control the front headlight (output 1, white wire) with F0 (both directions) and the rear headlight (output 2, yellow wire) with F3. To accomplish this, I leave CV33 programmed to 1. This means when the locomotive is moving forward, the front headlight is controlled with F0. Then I change CV34 from its default value (2) to 1. This allows the front headlight to be controlled by F0 when the locomotive is moving in reverse.

With the value changed, output 2 (the rear headlight in most decoders) is no longer controlled by anything. By reprogramming CV37 to 2, F3 now controls the rear headlight.

Function buttons can be programmed to control multiple function outputs at the same time. Since an eight-bit binary number can be any number between 0 and 255, you aren't limited to programming the CVs to only the values in the chart. To control multiple outputs, add the values for those outputs in the chart. If you want F2 (CV36) to control outputs 1, 3, and 8, add 1, 4, and 128, and program the value 133 into CV36.

Keep in mind that the function output values in the chart shift at function button F4. Output 1 can't be mapped to F4. If a value of 1 is programmed into CV38, F4 will control output 4, not output 1. The values shift again at F9.

These examples are only the NMRA recommendations, and not all decoder manufacturers map functions this way. Some decoders don't allow mapping at all. Those that do allow mapping typically use CVs 33-46, differing in the values for each column and at what function the values shift.

Some manufacturers, such as NCE, allow throttle buttons to be remapped. This is particularly useful on throttles that only have a few buttons. You can program those buttons to control the most-used functions and customize the button order to make it more convenient to operate.

Configuration variables for reprogramming														
Output	14	13	12	11	10	9	8	7	6	5	4	3	2	1
											Violet	Green	Yellow	White
Function button / CV														
F0 (forward) 33														D
F0 (reverse) 34													D	
F1 35												D		
F2 36											D			
F3 37										D				
F4 38										D				
F5 39									D					
F6 40								D						
F7 41							D							
F8 42						D								
F9 43					D									
F10 44				D										
F11 45			D											
F12 46		D												

1. Recommended configuration variables. The NMRA recommends using CVs 33 through 46 for reprogramming. Not all decoders use these CVs, and if they do, they may not use them the same way. The shaded boxes indicate values that aren't allowed.

How to program configuration variables														
Output	14	13	12	11	10	9	8	7	6	5	4	3	2	1
											Violet	Green	Yellow	White
Function button / CV														
F0 (forward) 33							128	64	32	16	8	4	2	1
F0 (reverse) 34							128	64	32	16	8	4	2	1
F1 35							128	64	32	16	8	4	2	1
F2 36							128	64	32	16	8	4	2	1
F3 37							128	64	32	16	8	4	2	1
F4 38				128	64	32	16	8	4	2	1			
F5 39				128	64	32	16	8	4	2	1			
F6 40				128	64	32	16	8	4	2	1			
F7 41				128	64	32	16	8	4	2	1			
F8 42				128	64	32	16	8	4	2	1			
F9 43	128	64	32	8	4	2	1							
F10 44	128	64	32	8	4	2	1							
F11 45	128	64	32	8	4	2	1							
F12 46	128	64	32	8	4	2	1							

2. Programming CVs. This chart shows a method many manufacturers use to program CVs in decoders. Not all manufacturers map functions this way, and some decoders don't have a mapping feature.

Using CV29

Configuration variable 29 (CV29) controls several locomotive functions. *Bill Zuback*

DCC allows independent control of several trains on the same track without dividing the layout into multiple isolated sections like DC cab control. In order to do that, each locomotive must contain a decoder programmed with a unique address so when a DCC system sends commands, they're directed only to a single locomotive or consist of engines.

A locomotive's programming is contained in a configuration variable, or CV. Some decoders have hundreds of CVs, while others only have a few. Decoders with back-electromotive-force control, lighting effects, and sound have more flexibility and more CVs. Configuration variables retain their value settings when power is removed from the decoder.

Even the locomotive address has some choices beyond its number. There are actually two addresses in almost all of today's decoders. One is the primary (two-digit) address, and the other is the extended (four-digit) address. The primary address is contained in CV1 and

the extended address is contained in CVs 17 and 18. The extended address requires two CVs to contain the four-digit number.

So how does the decoder know which address to respond to when a command is issued? That's where most people encounter CV29 for the first time.

Configuration variable 29, found in all decoders, is a special CV that activates a number of basic features, including which address is used. Configuration variables are 8 bits long. A bit is a single value, either 0 or 1. Digital engineers begin counting with the number 0, so the first bit (usually shown at the right of the number) is called bit 0 and has a weight of 1. If bit 0 is set to 1, and all the other bits are at a 0, then the entire value of CV 29 is 1.

The next bit is bit 1, and it has a weight of 2. If bit 1 is set to 1 and all other bits are a 0, then the entire value for CV 29 is 2. If bit 0 and bit 1 are both set to 1 then you add the bit weights (bit 0 = 1 and bit 1 = 2)

together, and the entire CV's value is 3. Each bit weight is twice the previous bit's weight, so bit 2's weight is 4, bit 4's weight is 8, and so forth until bit 7, the last of the 8 bits, is worth 128.

CV29 features

Configuration variable 29 controls several different features, and each bit of this CV controls a different aspect. If a 1 is placed in that bit (digital engineers call a value of 1 "set" and a value of 0 "clear"), that feature is turned on. By adding the weights of all the bits that are set (features turned on), a final number can be programmed into CV29 and the decoder's behavior will be known.

So what does each bit of CV29 control? Bit 0 controls locomotive direction. This doesn't mean that the DCC command station uses this bit to control which direction the locomotive runs in ordinary operation. Instead, bit 0 is used when initially installing the decoder.

On a wired decoder, the orange and

Configuration variables for reprogramming							
	Accessory decoder	Reserved	Addressing	Speed table	Bi-directional communication	Power source conversion	Headlight bit location	Direction
Bit number	7	6	5	4	3	2	1	0
Bit weight	128	64	32	16	8	4	2	1
Value	0	0	1	1	0	0	1	0

gray wires are connected to the motor. Sometimes it's not obvious which way the locomotive will run when a forward command is issued. If your locomotive runs in reverse, bit 0 can be set to reverse the polarity of the orange and gray wires.

Another application where bit 0 comes in handy is for locomotives that normally run long hood forward. If a drop-in or plug-and-play decoder is used in one of these locomotives, there is no way to reverse the direction of the range and gray wires, so the locomotive will run in reverse. Setting bit 0 will correct that.

Direction-sensitive functions, such as headlights, should also reverse when bit 0 is set, according to National Model Railroad Association recommendations. However, I've found some older decoders where that is not true.

Since CVs retain their value when power is removed, you should never have to change their value once the decoder is programmed. Bit 1 is a holdover from the early days of DCC when decoders used only 14 speed steps. The bit tells the decoder which DCC packet to search for the headlight information. Unless you're using 14 speed steps, this bit should be 1. If your DCC system is using 28 or 128 speed steps and this bit is set to 0, you may have erratic headlight performance.

Bit 2 controls power conversion. In the absence of DCC, this bit controls what system the decoder will respond to. When the locomotive is receiving valid DCC packets, the decoder continues to be controlled by those packets. But if bit 2 is set, the decoder may automatically switch to a different control system like Zero-1, CTC-16, or Railcommand. However, most DCC

decoders will not respond to other control systems. The control system the decoder will convert to is determined by the value of CV12, which is an optional CV. Most DCC decoders will respond to DC if CV29 bit 2 is set. This means if your locomotive is placed on the rails of a direct-current layout, it will function as if it were a DC locomotive.

This automatic conversion does carry some danger, however. During the startup of some DCC systems, power is present before valid DCC packets are sent. If bit 2 of CV29 is set, your locomotive may sense that as DC and take off at full speed. Unless you're planning to use automatic power conversion, it's best to clear bit 2.

Bit 3 enables bi-directional communication. This allows the decoder to send information back to the command station while the command station takes a "break" in sending DCC packets to the decoder. This break is called a cutout period. As of this writing, NMRA bi-directional communication has only seen limited use and isn't available in many DCC systems. Unless your system and decoder are capable of bi-directional communication, this bit should also be cleared.

Bit 4 enables a speed table, which allows for the customization of motor voltage for every speed step. This can be used for a number of things, but most often it's used for speed matching two or more locomotives (see pages 52-53). You may choose to program all your locomotives to operate at the same speed, or you may choose to differentiate by locomotive model.

For instance, a prototype yard engine usually loads (accelerates) more quickly than a road engine. Some decoders have a number of pre-

determined speed tables that usually include linear and logarithmic (exponential) curves. In these decoders, the value in CV25 determines which speed curve is used. In the decoder manual, there is normally a chart that indicates the optional speed curves enabled by CV25. If the decoder is capable of a speed curve but doesn't have a factory programmed one available, setting CV29 bit 4 automatically enables a user speed curve determined by CV67-CV94.

Bit 5 determines what type of address is active in the decoder. If bit 5 is set, the extended address is used.

Bit 6 is reserved by the NMRA for future use and is ignored by today's decoders. When calculating the value to program CV29, use 0 for bit 6.

Bit 7 should be cleared for locomotive decoders. This bit is also ignored by most decoders and should be set to 0.

To calculate the final value of CV29, it's best to fill in a chart like the one above. The chart tells us that the locomotive is in the normal (forward) direction and the headlights are set up for 28/128 speed steps. There is no automatic power conversion (DCC only) and no bi-directional communications. The speed table is enabled and the extended (four-digit) address is used. The value of CV29 is obtained by adding the appropriate bit weights 2 + 16 + 32 = 50.

The NMRA's recommended practice 9.2.2 dictates which features each bit controls so that all decoders respond the same way. Some DCC systems and some CV programming software automatically program CV29 to the value required by asking you a series of questions to determine what features you want. Once you get the hang of it, programming CV29 isn't difficult.

Adding sound

Many hobbyists strive to make their steam and diesel locomotive models look like the real thing. But those superb-looking models can be taken to the next level with sound.

Sound decoders have changed greatly in a short amount of time. Early decoders featured a generic library of steam or diesel locomotive sounds. Today's offerings are often based on recordings of full-size locomotives with well-rendered steam locomotive chuffs, diesel engine rumble, and prototype-specific air horns, steam whistles, and bells. Some companies offer downloadable sound files that can be used to customize a sound decoder.

Keep reading to see four sound decoder installation projects. With the right decoder and speaker, you can add sound to almost any locomotive.

How sound decoders work

Thanks to sound decoders, you can make model locomotives sound like their full-size counterparts. I'm often asked how they work. Recordings of prototype locomotives are used to reproduce the sounds. These recordings are converted into a format that can be stored within the decoder.

Sound consists of waves of various air pressures traveling through the air. The tone of the sound is determined by the frequency of the wave; the volume depends on the pressure level. A microphone converts sound waves into similar electrical waves. The frequency of the waves is the same as the frequency of the sound pressure waves. The pressure level (volume) is converted in the amplitude (voltage) of the electrical signal. The sound is still an analog signal at this point. It is converted to digital format using an analog-to-digital converter (ADC). This device measures the voltage at intervals called the sample rate. In order to reproduce the waveform later, the sample rate has to be at least twice the highest frequency of the recorded sound. Audible sound is in the range of 20 Hz to 20 kHz, so the sample rate of the ADC must be at least 40 kHz. In other words, a sample must be taken at least every 25 microseconds.

The rumble of diesel engines and the blast of an air horn are just a few prototype sounds we can add to our model locomotives. Mike explains how sound decoders work. *Cody Grivno*

The voltage measured by the ADC is expressed in a binary number of a certain amount of bits. A bit is either a 1 (a voltage level) or 0 (zero voltage). The more bits, the more faithful the digitized waveform will be to the original analog waveform. An example of a digitized waveform is atop the next page.

For example, let's say that the maximum analog voltage the ADC can digitize is +/- 2 volts (V) and the ADC is only 4 bits wide. Each bit is worth twice the value of the previous bit. With one bit, there are two different values, zero and one. With two bits, four different values can be determined by using a combination of the two bits like this: 00, 01, 10, and 11. With 4 bits, 16 different voltage levels can be determined.

Since the voltage range is +2V to -2V, that's a total of 4V, 2V above zero and 2V below zero. If you take the voltage range (4V) and divide it by the number of voltage levels (16) you get what's called the step size of the ADC. In this case, it's .25V. The smaller the step size, the more accurately the waveform is reproduced. If the actual voltage at a given sample time is 1.05V, the ADC would convert it as if it were 1V. If the step size was .05V instead of .25V, the ADC would convert it as 1.05, a more accurate number.

The files are stored in the decoder's digital memory. The sound decoder uses a microprocessor to convert the digital signal from the rails into commands for the motor and lighting. The decoder's microprocessor is also capable of converting the stored digital numbers into sound again.

The data is retrieved from the digital memory at the same sample rate used for the original conversion and run through a digital-to-analog converter (DAC). The DAC creates an analog voltage from the stored data. In our example, the original 1.05V signal was stored as a number that represented 1V. The DAC takes that number and creates a 1V signal. The 1V is then amplified and fed into a speaker that re-creates the sound.

Sampling

It's impractical to record hours of real locomotive sounds and store that into a sound decoder. Further, a prototype locomotive wouldn't be doing the same sequence of events that your model would be doing. Therefore, only snippets of different sounds are stored in the decoder. When they're played back, they're looped to make the sound continuous. There may only be a short recording of a diesel engine in notch 1. When played in a model, the decoder replays that sound until the throttle is moved to another position.

Sounds like a bell, whistle, or air horn are especially interesting. The sound isn't continuous. When the bell is struck, there is a sharp tone followed by ringing that gradually fades away. Sounds like this are divided into three parts: attack, sustain, and decay. These sounds are stored separately in the decoder until the microprocessor

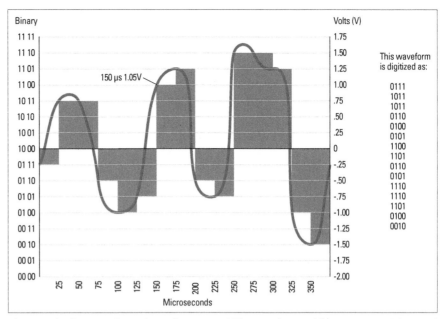

This graph of a waveform shows how sound files are digitized for use in a DCC sound decoder. This method of bit encoding is called offset binary.

Mike added the decoder and speaker for the steam engine in the tender. In the diesel, the decoder is above the motor and the speaker over the rear truck.

strings them together at the appropriate time. First is the attack. This is followed by the sustain, which is looped as long as needed. The toll ends with the decay.

Real locomotives, of course, produce many sounds at the same time. The generator whines while the safety valves pop or the bell rings while the air compressor runs. The processor is able to use different sound clips simultaneously and mix them together. The composite sound is sent to the amplifier and then to the speaker.

It isn't necessary to understand these inner workings unless you're using a decoder that allows you to download your own sound projects. Those decoders have software that allow you to piece together your own sound clips and control when they are played. You must have a computer and specialized hardware that allows you to download your sound projects into the decoder.

The following pages show you how to perform installations.

Two decoders for one locomotive

Mike added a motor decoder to this Kato HO scale SD40-2 model shortly after purchasing it, but he later upgraded the model with sound. Read on to see how Mike added a sound decoder and speaker to this six-axle road locomotive.

1 Mike used the Digitrax SFX004 Soundbug sound decoder in his SD40-2. The decoder includes a 28mm speaker, but it was too big, so he replaced it with a mini-oval speaker and enclosure from Tony's Train Exchange.

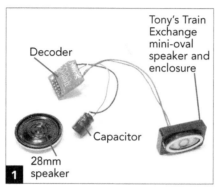

2 A notch in the weight above the locomotive's rear truck was all the room Mike needed to install the mini-oval speaker and enclosure. Mike decided to place the speaker facing downward.

If you're like me, you probably have several locomotives with DCC motor-only decoders. I wanted to add sound to a model like this, but was reluctant to remove the motor decoder because of the money and time I spent purchasing and programming it. Fortunately, the Kato HO scale SD40-2 shown above had room for both a motor decoder and sound decoder, so I was able to keep my NCE D14SR decoder and add a separate Digitrax sound decoder.

The NCE D14SR motor decoder plugs into the 8-pin socket on the Kato light board. A word of caution, though: One of the screws securing the light board and a plastic clip holding the power contacts must be removed for the NCE decoder to fit properly. If these items aren't removed, the shell won't seat correctly. I soldered the power contacts to the light board, eliminating the need for the plastic clip.

My Kato SD40-2 is from an early run that had electrical contact problems. There are a number of ways to correct this, including soldering a small wire from the nubs on the trucks to the long brass wipers on the chassis. No matter how you correct the problem, it's important that there's good electrical contact with the rails before the decoder is installed. If a locomotive doesn't run well on DC, it won't run well on DCC.

Location
I used the Digitrax SFX004 Soundbug sound-only decoder for the SD40-2, **1**. Probably the toughest part of any sound decoder installation is finding a place for the speaker, and the Kato model was no exception.

The Digitrax sound decoder comes with a 28mm-diameter speaker. This speaker was too big for the space I had available, so I looked for a smaller option. The decoder's manual says any speaker of at least 8Ω can be used, so I purchased a mini-oval speaker and enclosure from Tony's Train Exchange.

Speakers operate more efficiently and sound much better with an appropriate enclosure. You can either purchase a commercial enclosure or make

your own from styrene. Take accurate measurements of the area where you're going to install the speaker and enclosure. I put the SD40-2's speaker and enclosure at the rear of the hood, below the radiator fans. Be aware that the mini-oval speaker sticks out approximately .10" from the enclosure. The rear of the Kato drive has a notch in the weight where the enclosure can conveniently nest, **2**.

I placed the speaker face down. Then I drilled a small hole in the back of the enclosure, snaked the speaker wires through it, and soldered them to the speaker. I always clamp speakers to the workbench when soldering so the iron's tip doesn't accidentally attract the speaker's magnet.

Finally, I used electrical tape to secure the decoder directly in front of the speaker on top of the weight above the rear truck, **3**.

Wiring
The sound decoder can be directly attached to certain Digitrax motor decoders using two 2-56 screws and an

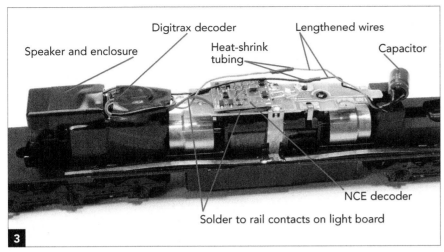

Speaker and enclosure — Digitrax decoder — Heat-shrink tubing — Lengthened wires — Capacitor — NCE decoder — Solder to rail contacts on light board

3

After hard-wiring the decoder in place, Mike secured the decoder to the weight with electrical tape. In order for the body shell to seat properly, he located the capacitor at the other end of the motor.

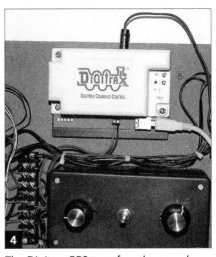

4

The Digitrax PR3 transfers the sound information from the computer to the decoder. The programmer must be connected to an isolated section of track.

8-pin connector. Digitrax also offers a drop-in motor decoder for later Kato SD40-2s that its Soundbug plugs into. The light-emitting diode headlights on this decoder aren't aligned properly for older Kato units like mine.

Since I was adding the sound decoder to a locomotive with another manufacturer's motor decoder, I had to wire it. Wiring the sound decoder couldn't have been simpler. It requires just two connections, one to each rail. The contacts for these connections are where the 2-56 screws attach. I soldered red and black 30AWG wires to the sound decoder at those locations (one wire to each contact). Then I soldered the wires to the rail contacts on the Kato light board, **3**. The rail contacts are the ones in the center of the light board, while the motor contacts are toward the front. No connections between the sound decoder and the motor contacts are necessary.

The sound decoder also has a factory-installed electrolytic capacitor. I placed it on the other side of the motor, behind the cab. However, I had to splice the wires to lengthen them, **3**. It's critical that the polarity of the capacitor is maintained. Before removing the capacitor from the original wires, make a note which color wire is attached to the negative lead of the capacitor. The negative lead is marked by a colored stripe with a minus sign

on it. If you're in doubt, mark the capacitor itself to note which wire goes where.

Once I completed the installation, I tested the sound decoder by placing my locomotive on the main line and selecting address 3. (All DCC decoders come from the factory programmed to address 3.) The speaker roared to life and I was able to test the horn and the bell.

Programming

The Digitrax website has a number of factory-programmed sound "projects," or packages, including one for the EMD SD40-2. I downloaded the file to the computer at my workbench. These sound projects can be modified or created with standard .wav files. Snippets of recordings of full-size locomotives can be patched together in predetermined locations using the Digitrax SoundLoader program, available as a free download from the manufacturer's website.

A special Digitrax programmer is needed to transfer the sound projects from a computer to the decoder. If you have an older computer with a standard serial port, use the PR2 programmer. Computers equipped with USB ports require the PR3, seen in **4**. There are commercial USB-to-serial port converters that allow the PR2 to work on USB ports. However, Digitrax warns

that some converters aren't compatible with the PR2.

The Digitrax programmer must be connected to an isolated piece of track. I connected mine to the programming track on my workbench.

To prevent any interaction between the motor and sound decoders during programming, I removed the NCE decoder. Then I followed the instructions for downloading the SD40-2 sound project into the decoder. I programmed the address of the sound decoder to the engine's road number.

I reinstalled the motor decoder and tested it with the sound decoder. Any further programming of configuration variables will affect both decoders. The NCE decoder is easy to remove, so I can program it separately using the firm's decoder tester. To adjust the remaining Digitrax decoder I use the programming track.

Some decoders have a locking feature, preventing them from being programmed until they're unlocked. This allows two decoders on the programming track to be programmed independently.

After running my Kato SD40-2 in silence, I can now enjoy listening to the rumble of a 645E3 diesel engine, ringing the bell, and blowing the horn at grade crossings. Now my locomotive not only operates like its full-size counterpart, but it sounds like it too.

Sound for N scale F units

By David Popp

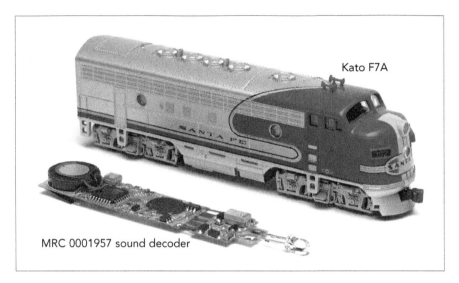

Kato F7A

MRC 0001957 sound decoder

I happen to have Kato's *El Capitan* passenger train, and I thought it would be fun to run it on *Model Railroader's* Salt Lake Route N scale project layout. (For more on that railroad, see the January 2010 MR.) To do that, I needed to convert the train's EMD F7 diesels to DCC. While I was at it, I thought it would be great to add sound as well. Model Rectifier Corp. makes a drop-in sound decoder for these

models (no. 0001957), so I purchased a couple of them from Tony's Train Exchange and got to work.

Model Rectifier calls this particular item a "snap-in" decoder, and for the most part, that's what the installation turned out to be—a snap. I had the decoders installed and running in an hour, and it would have been less if I hadn't had to stop to photograph the work. Photos **1** to **5** show the steps.

Programming

Once I had the decoders in the models and tested them, it was time to do a little programming, starting with the address. I used an NCE Corp. Power Cab DCC system to do all the work, and I found that when programming the MRC decoders on the main, I didn't always get the decoder to take the new configuration variable (CV) values. However, by switching to the programming track, I was able to get the results I wanted on the first try. Your programming results could vary, depending upon the DCC system you use. First, I changed the locomotive addresses. I used the cab number for the F7A, which was 302. The Kato F7Bs come unnumbered, so after a quick bit of researching, I chose 300B. Digital Command Control manufacturers haven't figured out how to put letters into addresses yet, so I just used 300, writing the address on the bottom of the fuel tank.

Next, I experimented with various sound settings. The MRC decoder comes with 6 different prime mover

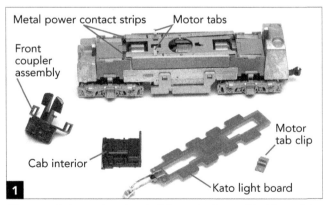

1 Front coupler assembly — Metal power contact strips — Motor tabs — Cab interior — Kato light board — Motor tab clip

After gently loosening the shell from the frame, David carefully worked the coupler through the opening in the pilot and set the shell aside. He then removed the motor tab clip, the cab interior, and the Kato light board. Since the front coupler assembly is delicate, he carefully removed it from the frame and set it aside as well. *Bill Zuback photos*

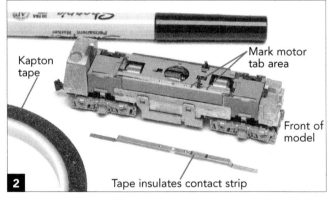

2 Kapton tape — Mark motor tab area — Front of model — Tape insulates contact strip

To isolate the motor, David first marked the location of the motor tabs on the power contact strips. He then removed one strip at a time and covered the marked area with Kapton tape to insulate it from the motor tabs. Be sure the tape covers the bottom, outside edge, and top of the strip.

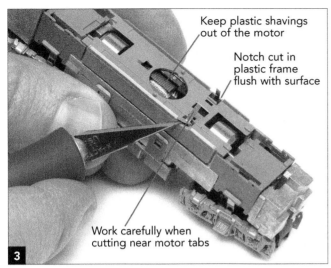

Keep plastic shavings out of the motor

Notch cut in plastic frame flush with surface

Work carefully when cutting near motor tabs

3

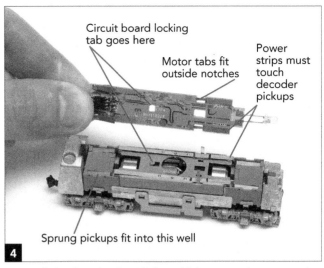

Circuit board locking tab goes here

Motor tabs fit outside notches

Power strips must touch decoder pickups

Sprung pickups fit into this well

4

Following MRC's installation instructions, David cut notches in the plastic frame next to the motor tabs as shown above. The notches make it easier for the motor tabs to fit properly around the taped contact strips. The soft plastic is easy to cut with a sharp knife, but be careful to keep the shavings out of the open motor and don't damage the motor tabs.

To install the decoder, David slipped it between the motor tabs and positioned the circuit-board locking tab in the appropriate opening. He then slid the decoder to the back of the locomotive for the tab to engage and hold it in place. Be sure to check your work: The contact strips must fit flush with the pickup pads on the bottom of the decoder.

sounds, which are set using CV123. I set CV123 to a value of 5, which is MRC's version of an EMD 567 diesel engine. The decoder also includes 23 different horns (CV51) and 16 different bells (CV52). After trying several, I decided I liked the default settings the best, which were a value of 13 for the horn and 3 for the bell. I lowered the bell volume by setting CV53 to a value of 12.

Consisting, speed matching

I used the advanced consisting function (CV19) to set up my F units to run together in multiple unit sets. This is a great feature because it allows me to run the Fs together on any layout's DCC system. See page 54 for more on advance consisting.

First, I programmed CV19 in both units to the consist address. This has to be a value between 0 and 127. I used address 33 for my Santa Fe F units, and I wrote it on the bottom of their fuel tanks for future reference.

Next I programmed CV21 in F7A 302, the lead engine, to a value of 1. This allows all of the engine's button-activated functions to operate while in the consist, so I can turn the headlight on and off, ring the bell, and blow the horn without having to switch my DCC throttle to the engine's road number to do it.

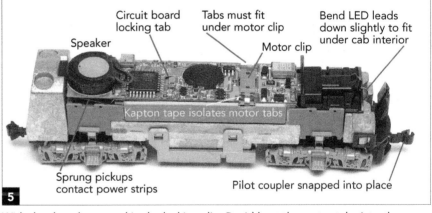

Circuit board locking tab

Speaker

Tabs must fit under motor clip

Motor clip

Bend LED leads down slightly to fit under cab interior

Kapton tape isolates motor tabs

Sprung pickups contact power strips

Pilot coupler snapped into place

5

With the decoder seated in the locking clip, David bent the motor tabs into the center of the locomotive and secured them with the plastic motor clip. The tabs need to contact the designated pads on the decoder for the motor to operate. After checking the locomotive ran properly on a test track, he reassembled the model as shown above. For the cab interior to fit properly, the leads on the LED headlight need to be bent downward slightly.

After separating the two engines but still running them as a consist, I found that engine 302 would start moving at step 2 while running in 128 speed steps, but unit 300 wouldn't start until speed step 8. When set to speed step 16, the units ran fairly close to even, so it was just a starting voltage issue in engine 300.

To fix the problem, I programmed CV2 in unit 300 with a higher starting voltage. I tried successively higher values, working initially by 10s, and tested the results until the engine

began running at step 2. It turned out that I needed a value of 55 in CV2, which did the trick. Both models now perform well together.

There was a time when I thought N scale sound decoders would never get to the point of where they both sounded good and were fun to use. Thanks to today's better, easier-to-install decoders, I've changed my opinion on that front. Now that I have my F units set up for DCC and sound, it's time for them to take the *El Cap* for a spin through the desert!

Add sound to a modern diesel

By Michael Asmussen

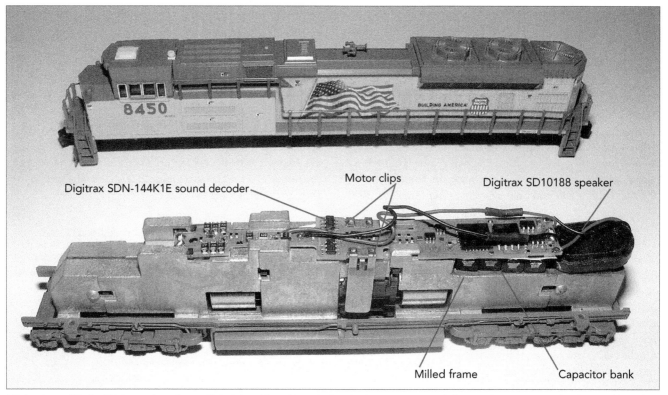

Digitrax SDN-144K1E sound decoder — Motor clips — Digitrax SD10188 speaker — Milled frame — Capacitor bank

Michael modified a Digitrax decoder to fit inside a Kato N scale SD70ACe. His easy-to-follow techniques can also be used on the firm's **SD70MAC**. *Michael Asmussen*

Dremel no. 199 high-speed cutting disk

.080"

1

To make room for the speaker and capacitor, Michael milled .080" from the frame with a Dremel high-speed cutting bit. *Jim Forbes*

I'm in the process of building my version of the N scale Salt Lake Route, *Model Railroader's* 2010 project layout. I want to have a fleet of sound-equipped locomotives operating trains on the layout, but none of the models I want are available with factory-equipped sound. I chose to use a Digitrax SDN-144K1E sound decoder, and with a bit of modification I was able to install it in my Kato EMD SD70ACe (these modifications will also work the firm's SD70MAC).

The SDN-144K1E is designed for the Kato SD40-2 and General Electric Evolution-series locomotives. However, the speaker and capacitor won't fit inside a Kato SD70ACe or SD70MAC. The fuel tank on these models is too shallow to mount a

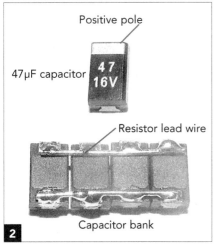

Positive pole

47µF capacitor

47 16V

Resistor lead wire

Capacitor bank

2

Michael replaced the round capacitor with four 47µF surface-mount capacitors. He glued them together before soldering them together. *Michael Asmussen*

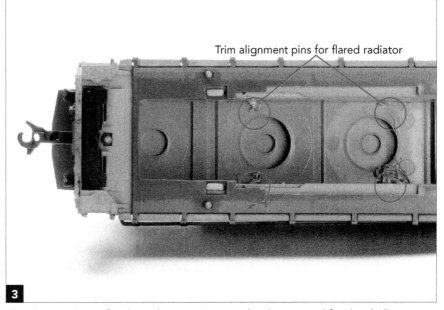

Trim alignment pins for flared radiator

3

The alignment pins for the radiator section need to be trimmed for the shell to seat properly. Michael used flush cutters, but a chisel blade will also work. *Jim Forbes*

speaker in, and the round capacitor won't fit under the shell.

I resolved the speaker issue by using a Digitrax SP10188, which measures 10mm x 18mm. I used Jaycar Electronics RZ6574 47µF (microfarad) surface-mount capacitors, which fit well under the Digitrax decoder. Equivalent capacitors for readers in North America are Digi-Key 399-5215-1-ND.

Installation

I started the installation by lifting off the press-fit shell and disassembling the mechanism. To make room for the replacement speaker and capacitor, I used a Dremel no. 199 high-speed cutting bit and a metal grinding disk to mill .080" from the rear of the frame, **1**. It's important to wear eye protection during this step. The cutting bit and grinding disk throw off small pieces of metal. I cleaned off any metal filings, as these can potentially damage the motor.

Next, I unsoldered the 13mm round speaker supplied with the Digitrax decoder. Before connecting the replacement, I shortened the leads to remove the excess wire. The polarity isn't important, as one speaker can't be out of phase.

I then turned my attention to the capacitor. On the Digitrax website, it says the capacitor is 330µF, but the manual clearly shows it's 100µF. The

100µF capacitor doesn't have enough capacitance to be used reliably with all DCC systems. The replacement bank is made up of four 47µF surface-mount capacitors with a minimum rating of 16V. This results in a smoother running engine.

I glued the capacitors together so they wouldn't slide apart while I soldered them, **2**. I made sure the positive polarity markers were on the same side before soldering them together with cut-off resistor leads. I cut the red and black wires off the Digitrax capacitor and extended the leads on the new capacitors with the excess speaker wire I'd removed earlier.

When soldering the capacitor bank, polarity is important. The positive side, which has a colored band, is connected to the red wire from the decoder. I applied Kapton tape to the top of the bank so it wouldn't cause a short if it touched the printed-circuit board.

I reassembled the motor, frame, and trucks and reinstalled the fuel tank cover. Then I set the Digitrax sound decoder into place. The power-pickup pads are at the front of the decoder. They need to make solid contact with the top of the frame.

The printed-circuit (PC) board for the Digitrax decoder is a bit thinner than the Kato DC light board, so it makes poor contact with the frame.

To remedy this, I placed a plastic shim under the board near the motor tabs. The PC board is delicate, so the shim shouldn't be too thick. I found .040" or less to be sufficient. The goal is to bend the board slightly so pressure is applied to the pickup pads.

Before I replaced the motor clips, I put two more pieces of Kapton tape on the sides of the frame to prevent a short circuit. Then I tested the sound decoder to make sure it functioned properly. Much to my delight, it worked as advertised.

In order for the shell to seat properly, I removed the four pins for the flared radiator, **3**. I used flush cutters, but a chisel blade in a hobby knife will also work.

The decoder comes with factory-installed sounds for an SD40. I went to the Digitrax website (www.digitrax.com) to get the sound file for an SD70ACe. Once I had that installed, I changed CV58 to 15 to increase the volume and CV11 to 00 to make the sound continue when the locomotive is idling.

Within a few hours after starting the project, I was able to enjoy the realism of a sound-equipped SD70ACe. The project requires some patience, but in the end you'll be rewarded with a good-looking—and sounding—modern locomotive.

Modern sound for an old locomotive

Mike wanted the decoder functions on the superdetailed F3, right, kitbashed by a friend, to match its appearance, so he replaced the old NCE decoder with a SoundTraxx Tsunami.

My friend, the late Mark Simonson, kitbashed an old HO Athearn F7 into an F3, superdetailed it, and painted it for my favorite road, the Soo Line. When he gave me the locomotive about 15 years ago, I installed a basic NCE decoder, which, at the time, was state of the art. By today's standards, however, it's very noisy. The locomotive had non-lighted lenses for the headlight and red oscillating light. I decided it was time to update the decoder and lighting to match the modeling and detail work Mark had done.

I also wanted to add sound, so I chose a Soundtraxx Micro-Tsunami with EMD 567 prime mover sound.

Older Athearn locomotives have a metal clip that takes track power from one rail through a metal tab on the top of each truck and connects to the top side of the motor. The other side of the motor is connected to the frame, which makes contact to the other rail via a metal portion of the truck in direct contact with the frame under the gear tower.

Mark had installed a can motor, removed the clip, and wired the metal tabs directly to one motor lead. He drilled and tapped a 2-56 hole in the frame, put a screw in it, and soldered the wire to the other motor lead to the top of the screw. He mounted the motor on a layer of silicone adhesive, isolating it from the frame (a necessity when installing a DCC decoder).

The can motor improved slow-speed running and reduced the current draw. Any DCC decoder must be able to supply more current than the locomotive's motor will draw at a stall. In this case, the can motor draws about 400 mA and the Micro-Tsunami is capable of supplying 750 mA (including lighting). That meant I had about 350 mA left over for lighting—more than enough for both lights.

I soldered an 18AWG red wire between the two metal tabs above the gear tower and connected the decoder's red wire to one of the tabs. The wire between the tabs must be flexible enough to allow suitable movement of the trucks. Stranded wire is more flexible than solid wire. The decoder's black wire was soldered to the screw in the frame.

The orange and gray wires from the decoder were soldered to the motor leads. The orange wire is connected to the positive side of the motor, which, in a DC locomotive, is connected to the right hand rail as viewed from above when the locomotive is traveling forward. The gray wire is connected to the negative motor terminal. If you get this backward, it's easy to fix by adding the value of 1 to the value in configuration variable (CV) 29.

Lighting

The prototype for my locomotive had a red oscillating light at the top of the nose and a white headlight in the front door. I wanted the lighting to be similar in appearance to my Athearn Genesis F units. I used light-emitting diodes (LEDs) for both. I chose a Miniatronics Yeloglo white 3mm LED for the headlight and a red Kingbright 3mm LED (www.mouser.com) for the oscillating light.

LEDs need a current-limiting resistor wired in series with the decoder function output. Some LEDs have them pre-wired into the leads, and some decoders have a resistor built into the function, usually a 1KΩ, but the Tsunami does not. If the decoder manual doesn't explicitly say the decoder has a resistor, you must add one.

I used Evergreen ³⁄₁₆" styrene tubing

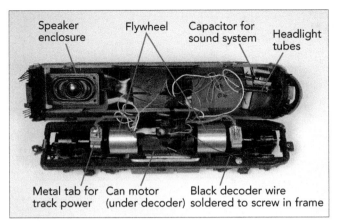

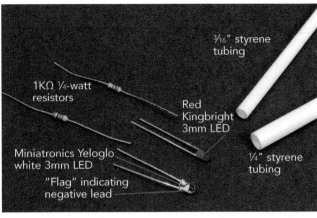

Mike had plenty of room inside the Athearn F unit for the decoder, speaker, and lights.

Mike used LEDs with 1KΩ resistors mounted in styrene tubing for the headlight and oscillating red light.

to make holders for the LEDs. The slope of the nose prevents the 3/16" tube from fitting flush with the back of the upper headlight opening. To prevent light leaks, I cut a shorter length of 1/4" tubing sliced in half lengthwise so that it was half-round, filed it to match the slope of the nose, and glued it to the bottom of the holder.

Everything was painted black to further reduce light leaks. When the paint was dry, I glued the parts in place.

In order to slip the LED into the tube, I had to file a lip off the base of the LED. I chucked the lens of the LED into the drill press for my motor-tool and, using eye protection, ran it at the slowest setting and used a sharp file to remove the lip.

I tested the LEDs with a 12VDC power supply and chose a 1KΩ 1/4-watt resistor to mimic the brightness of my Genesis Fs. Page 74 has more detail about choosing headlight resistors.

The 1KΩ resistors are wired in series with function leads (one on the white wire and one on the yellow wire) of the decoder and are soldered to the negative side of the LEDs. The blue wire is soldered to the positive lead of both LEDs.

The white wire controls the front headlight and the yellow wire normally controls the rear headlight, but since my F3 doesn't have a rear headlight, I used the yellow wire to control the oscillating light.

LEDs must be wired with the correct polarity or they won't light. Often, the longest lead is positive or there's a flat spot on the lens by the nega-

tive lead. I've found the most reliable method is to look into the LED from the side and look for a little "flag." That indicates the negative side.

The Micro-Tsunami has a capacitor to help prevent interruption of sound over dirty track. The positive side of the capacitor is connected to the blue lighting function wire and the negative side to the green/yellow wire.

I mounted a rectangular speaker and speaker enclosure inside the rear of the shell using double-sided foam tape and connected it to the purple wires on the decoder. I usually use the biggest speaker I can get into the space and use an enclosure to improve the sound quality and increase the volume. Cover all bare wires with heat-shrink tubing.

I placed the locomotive on my programming track and read back the value of CV1, the decoder's short address. You should get a value of 3, the factory setting. This indicates everything is wired correctly. I programmed the decoder's long address to 202 to match the locomotive number.

Because of the low current of the programming track, it's less likely to cause damage in case of a mistake. But some systems have trouble reading CVs from sound decoders. A programming booster such as the SoundTraxx PTB-100 can solve this.

The documentation in the decoder packaging only contains the basics of wiring and some basic CV programming, so I needed to consult the Tsunami Diesel Sound User's Guide from its website (www.soundtraxx. com). I wanted the headlight (white

wire) to light in either forward or reverse. Most decoders auto-reverse the headlight and rear headlight depending on the direction of the locomotive.

I programmed both CV33 and CV34 to a value of 1, which made the F0 button on my throttles control the headlight regardless of direction. I programmed CV35 to a value of 2 so F1 would control the oscillating headlight. This required moving the bell function that is normally controlled by F1 to F3 by programming CV37 to a value of 1.

To make the headlight dimmable with F7, I programmed CV49 to a 1, but, since the headlight is an LED, SoundTraxx provides an additional value of 128 to add to the value of CV49 to make dimming more realistic. That makes the total value programmed into CV49 a 129.

I simulated the oscillating headlight by programming CV50 (corresponds with the yellow wire) to 135. That's the sum of SoundTraxx's Hyperlight mode setting (7) for a rotary beacon and the LED setting (128). The Hyperlight modes can be found in Table G on page 33 of the Tsunami Diesel Sound User's Guide. There are many different Hyperlight modes, but I found this one to be most like my Athearn Genesis locomotives.

I changed the horn setting to the signal chime "blat" horn by setting CV115 to a value of 1.

Updating Mark's locomotive was a fun project, and I enjoy seeing his handiwork running on my layout with my other locomotives.

Lighting for all occasions

Prototype locomotives have headlights, ditch lights, oscillating warning lights, and in some instances, classification lights. Passenger and commuter cars have lit interiors and marker lights. On many railroads, traffic is governed by illuminated signals.

But how can we add those full-size lighting effects to our scale models? We'll take a look at locomo-tive headlights, ditch lights, Mars lights, and rotary beacons. Then we'll shift our focus to the rear of the train by looking at interior lighting and marker lights for cabooses. Next, we'll explore how to light bi-level gallery cars and passenger car interiors. Then we'll wrap things up with a story on how to control train-order signals.

Headlights and DCC

Bulb and LED headlights can easily be controlled with DCC. *Bill Zuback photos*

1 Older Athearn (and many other) locomotives, such as this SD40-2, featured large 12-18V light bulbs.

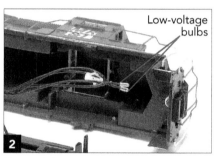

Low-voltage bulbs

2 Newer Athearn SD40-2s are among many locomotives that use small, low-voltage bulbs.

Working headlights not only make locomotives look realistic, but can add to the realism of operation. Using headlights in a prototypical manner is one of the easiest things to do with Digital Command Control (DCC).

Almost every decoder has function outputs that are controlled by buttons on a throttle. These outputs can be wired to a locomotive's headlights and configured to not only turn the headlight on and off, but make it dim, flash, and do a host of other special effects.

Wiring

On wired decoders the blue wire is the lighting common, which is a positive voltage. The white, yellow, green, and purple wires are the function outputs. The outputs are a high impedance (no voltage) when off, and usually 1 volt (V) above ground when on. When the headlight is on, current flows from the blue wire through the headlight and returns to the function output.

The voltage between the blue wire and the function output wire is typically 1V or so less than track voltage. Track voltage is usually 14V but can vary, especially in DCC systems designed for larger scales.

The best way to determine function voltage is to measure it with a DC voltmeter. Connect the red and black decoder wires to the track, select the decoder with the throttle (address 3 is used on new decoders until it's changed), set the direction forward, and turn on the headlight with the throttle's function button. Use the voltmeter to measure the voltage across the white and blue wires.

From the factory, function button zero (F0) controls the front (white wire) and rear (yellow wire) headlights. When the locomotive is traveling forward, the front headlight is lit. In reverse, the rear headlight is on. This isn't the way headlights work on full-size locomotives, so some decoders allow you to program the front and rear lights independently using configuration variables (CVs). With function mapping, you can program a decoder to change which function button on your DCC system controls a specific output wire.

There are often restrictions with function mapping. You may not be able to assign certain function buttons to a specific output. Configuration variables can also vary between brands of decoders, so consult the instruction manual.

Light bulbs

Decoders can power both light bulbs and light-emitting diodes (LEDs). Bulbs come in a variety of sizes and voltages. How they're wired depends on the voltage and current of the bulb.

Older locomotives often have 12-18V bulbs, **1**. If the bulb is connected directly across the motor or rails of a DC locomotive, it's a 12-18V bulb. As built, the brightness of these bulbs varies with the speed of the locomotive.

Most of the time, light bulbs can be driven directly by a DCC decoder function output. You should test the bulb by powering it off a DC power pack to measure the voltage across and current through the bulb when it's operating at full brightness.

To measure the bulb's voltage, connect a multimeter across the bulb and slowly turn up the power pack until the bulb is at the desired brightness. To measure current, connect the multimeter in series with one of the bulb leads and set the meter to current (milliamps). This may require moving a lead of the meter to another jack. Turn the DC power pack to the same spot as you did to measure the voltage and note the current reading.

A bulb's brightness is dependent on the voltage applied. If the function output provides a lower voltage than you want, you'll have to use another bulb. If you run the bulb on a voltage lower than its maximum, it will last longer.

You can't use a bulb that draws more current than the function output is rated to deliver. The function output current rating is usually listed on the decoder packaging or in the manual.

Newer locomotives are typically equipped with lower-voltage bulbs, **2**. These locomotives have light boards with diodes that provide a constant voltage to the bulbs. Measuring the voltage across the bulb is the most reliable way to determine its voltage, but this task can be difficult with very low voltage bulbs. I keep a 1.5V AA battery at my workbench that I use to test for 1.5V bulbs. If the bulb lights at normal brightness with the battery, then it's a 1.5V bulb. If it doesn't light or lights dimly, it requires a higher voltage.

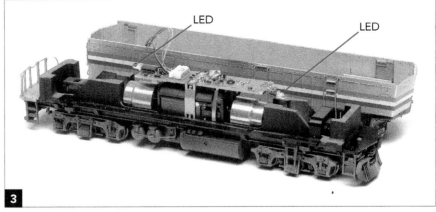

This Kato HO scale EMD F40PH uses LED headlights. Light from the diodes is directed to the headlights via a clear plastic bar inside the shell.

It may be possible to trace out the light board and count the number of diodes across the bulb. If you can do that with certainty, multiply the number of diodes by 0.7V (the voltage drop of a silicon diode) and that will be the approximate voltage of the bulb. Keep in mind that there may be more diodes on the light board than are used for a single bulb.

To operate lower-voltage bulbs with a function output, a voltage-dropping resistor must be wired in series between the output and the bulb.

To calculate the value of the resistor, use Ohm's Law ($V = I \times R$) and a little algebra. The value of V is the voltage you want to drop. That will be the function voltage minus the bulb voltage. The current of the bulb (I) is measured in milliamps (mA), and R is the value of the resistor in kilohms (KΩ).

For example, if you have a 12V function and a 1.5V bulb that draws 15 mA, the formula would be (12-1.5)/15, or 0.7KΩ (700Ω). Always use the next standard resistor value above the calculated value. In this case, for a 5-percent-tolerance resistor, that is 750Ω. As a check, the value of the resistor is usually somewhere between 100Ω and 1,000Ω. NCE has a chart for 1.5V bulbs in its decoder manual to make your calculation easier.

The next resistor property to determine is power dissipation, measured in watts (W). The formula is $P = V \times I$ or $P = I^2 \times R$. In the example above, the calculation would be 15mA x 15mA x 750, or 168mW. Always use a resistor the next size up, in this case ¼W.

The closer the power dissipation is to the resistor rating, the hotter the resistor will get. Use a larger resistor if you have room.

The dropping resistor can be connected to the function wire or the common (blue) wire. However, avoid using a single resistor for all the bulbs connected to the common wire. Should a bulb burn out, the current draw will drop. This may cause too much voltage to be applied to the other bulbs, burning them out as well.

LEDs

LEDs, **3**, are current driven. The more current that passes through the LED, the brighter it shines. As with lower-voltage light bulbs, LEDs also use a resistor in series with the function wire. However, the resistor is used here to limit the current. The calculation for the resistor value is the same as for a voltage-dropping resistor for bulbs. The forward voltage drop across an LED varies, but it's typically 3 to 4V.

A bulb can be connected with either lead connected to the blue wire, but LEDs only conduct current in one direction. The anode (positive) lead must be connected to the common wire. The current-limiting resistor can be connected on either side of the LED, but I always put it between the cathode (negative) lead and the function output. The cathode of the LED typically has a flat spot or is the shorter wire lead.

Don't let the formulas shown above intimidate you. Wiring headlights isn't difficult, and they'll add another dimension to your operating sessions.

An Athearn SD70ACe LED upgrade

By Pelle Soeborg

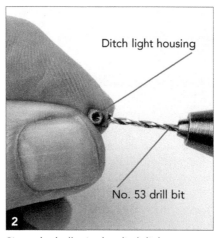

Run bead of silicone around edge of enclosure before securing speaker

Fill gap with .020" styrene

1

Pelle filled the opening at the bottom of the speaker enclosure with .020" styrene. Then he ran a bead of silicone around the edge of the enclosure before pressing the speaker into place.

Ditch light housing

No. 53 drill bit

2

Since the bulbs in the ditch light housings are secured with glue, Pelle had to use a no. 53 drill bit to crush the bulbs. He used a reamer to remove any glass and wire fragments.

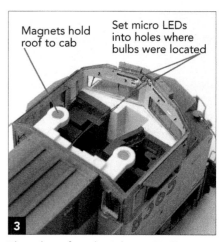

Magnets hold roof to cab

Set micro LEDs into holes where bulbs were located

3

The cab roof on the Athearn SD70ACe is secured with magnets. Pelle set the LEDs into the holes where the bulbs used to be located. Later, Pelle made new lens covers for the headlights with Microscale Kristal Klear.

When I acquired trio of older Athearn HO scale Electro-Motive Division SD70ACe diesel locomotives, I was a bit disappointed to find the models had bulbs for headlights instead of light-emitting diodes (LEDs). Some of the bulbs were so weak that you could hardly see them when they were illuminated. Since I had to remove the shell to replace the bulbs, I also sealed the speaker housing to improve the sound quality.

I started by removing the draft-gear boxes and two screws located under the trucks near the fuel tank. This allowed the shell to slide off easily.

Before replacing the lights, I worked on the speaker enclosure. The enclosure on the SD70ACe has an opening in the bottom (this issue was fixed on later Athearn SD70ACe models). After removing the speaker and enclosure, I filled the opening by attaching a piece of .020" styrene with cyanoacrylate adhesive (CA), **1**. Then I ran a bead of silicone along the edge of the enclosure

before reinstalling the speaker. The effect was dramatic, greatly improving the speaker's sound.

I replaced the bulbs with golden white micro-light-emitting diodes (LEDs) from Richmond Controls. On the surface this may sound easy, but care is required, especially when removing the ditch light housings from the platform. I gently twisted the housings from side to side until the glue joint broke. Since the bulbs are glued inside the housings (on newer models, the bulbs aren't glued in place), I wasn't able to pull them out by the wires. Instead, I used a drill bit to crush the bulbs inside the housings and used a reamer to remove the remaining fragments, **2**. I removed the clear plastic lenses with a thin metal pin to clear the bulb and glue residue stuck in the top of each housing.

I then inserted a LED in each housing. Before securing the LEDs with CA, make sure they're facing the right direction and you can see them

through the lens hole. After reattaching the lenses, I glued the ditch lights back on the platform with CA.

Replacing the front and rear headlights was a bit easier. The cab roof is held on with magnets, providing good access to the headlights. I glued the micro LEDs in the holes where the bulbs were located, **3**.

I attached the LEDs for the rear headlights to a small piece of styrene before attaching them to the shell. I drilled two small holes in the styrene and pulled the wires through the holes. Then I attached the LEDs with CA, **4**. I glued the light module so the LEDs were seated in the holes formerly occupied by the bulbs.

Wiring

With the LEDs in place, it was now time to attach them to the decoder. Resistors are required between each LED's common wire and the decoder's common output. I made a cluster with six 5.1KΩ resistors that fit inside above

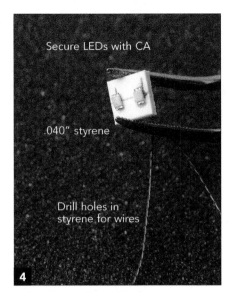

Secure LEDs with CA

.040" styrene

Drill holes in styrene for wires

4

Pelle attached the LEDs for the rear headlights to .040" styrene with cyano-acrylate adhesive. He drilled holes in the plastic so could pull the wires through.

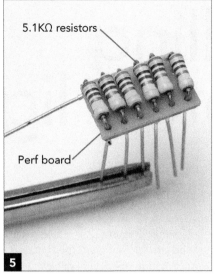

5.1KΩ resistors

Perf board

5

A 5.1KΩ resistor must be placed between each LED's common wire and the decoder's common output. The cluster fits above the rear truck.

the rear of the mechanism, as shown in **5**. To ensure a strong electrical connection, I soldered the leads to the decoder.

Photo **6** shows how I connected the LEDs to the decoder. There are a couple of options: if you want the ditch lights to flash in an alternating pattern when the air horn sounds, connect one LED to FX5 and the other to FX6. If you want the lights to remain in a constant "on" state, attach both to FX5.

You can see the finished installation in **7**. There was a bit of free space near the rear of the mechanism above the truck, so I set the cluster of resistors there and secured it with electrical tape. I also bundled the wires with electrical tape so they wouldn't get caught in the mechanism.

Finally, I slid the shell back on the chassis, being careful not to damage the sand lines. I learned this lesson the hard way after permanently damaging two lines. Then I used small dabs of Microscale Kristal Klear, applied carefully with the end of a paper clip, to make lenses for the front and rear headlights, **8**.

If you have early Athearn SD70ACe diesel locomotives like mine, sealing the speaker housing and replacing the light bulbs with LEDs will help make an already outstanding model even better.

Micro LED ditch light

Micro LED headlights

Micro LED ditch light

FX6 FX5

Headlight

Common output

Rear light

5.1kΩ resistors

Micro LED rear lights

6

This diagram shows how Pelle connected the light-emitting diodes (LEDs) to the decoder. Pelle attached the LEDs for the ditch lights to FX5 and FX6 so they flash in an alternating pattern when the air horn is sounded. If you want the headlights to remain constant, attach both to FX5.

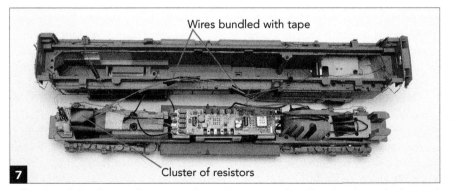

Wires bundled with tape

Cluster of resistors

7

Pelle placed the cluster of resistors above the rear truck and secured it with electrical tape. He also neatly wrapped the wires for the LEDs so they wouldn't get caught in the mechanism.

8

Pelle made lenses for the front and rear headlights with Microscale Kristal Klear. This comes out of the bottle milky, as shown above, but dries clear.

Controlling locomotive lighting

Besides controlling your locomotive's movement and sound, DCC also lets you control a variety of lighting effects. Just about every kind of light you see on a full-size locomotive can be duplicated on a model.

Prototype lighting

In addition to the front and rear headlights, prototype locomotives have numerous other lights you may not be aware of. Modern diesels are equipped with ditch lights (Canadian locomotives have had them for years) that can alternately flash when the air horn is blown. Diesels from earlier eras had oscillating signal lights (Mars lights or Gyralites) and rotating rooftop beacons. Platform lights, cab lights, and step lights have been features on diesels since their early days.

Lighting effects aren't just for diesels. Steam locomotives were almost always equipped with classification lights and sometimes signal lights, and the tenders had marker lights. Although not a light, per se, the glow of the firebox was often visible at night.

Digital Command Control decoders power lighting effects through function outputs. These outputs are activated by the throttle's function buttons, and Configuration Variables (CVs) determine how these functions work.

The term "function" is sometimes confusing because it refers to both an actual wire (or terminal) on the decoder and the buttons on a throttle. Not all decoders have a full range of outputs. If you want three different lighting effects on a locomotive, you must use a decoder with at least three function outputs.

Each function output consists of a single wire or terminal. A common wire is used for all functions to complete the circuit. On most decoders, the blue wire is common, per National Model Railroad Association Recommended Practice 9.1.1. It's usually around 12-14 volts (V).

The function output is actually a ground connection when the function is on. Some newer decoders have a +5V common for use with low-voltage light bulbs and light-emitting diodes (LEDs). A smaller resistor is needed for these lights.

Most decoders use two function outputs to control the headlights—one for the front and one for the rear. The default setting for the headlight control is F0. When the locomotive is moving forward, the front headlight is on. When the locomotive is in reverse, the rear headlight is illuminated.

On a full-size locomotive, the engineer controls which headlight is on. In some cases, such as yard engines, both are on at the same time. Because of this, I reprogram my decoders to use F0 to control the front headlight and another function button to control the rear, regardless of direction. This is called "function mapping." Not all decoders allow function mapping, and even if they do, they may not allow all of the outputs to be mapped to all of the function buttons.

Ditch lights also require two function outputs if you want them to flash alternately. The common wire is connected to both ditch lights and two function outputs are connected, one to each light.

Over the years, there have been a number of different lights used on prototype locomotives. For example, a strobe light is an electronic device that flashes suddenly to full brightness and shuts off just as suddenly. Some locomotives have two strobe lights, used to get the attention of motorists, that alternately flash. Other strobes flash twice in rapid succession, then pause.

Another type of light found on locomotives from the 1960s through the 1990s is a rotary beacon. These lights, used to locate engines in yards, slowly get bright and slowly dim.

Effects programming

There are DCC decoders that can simulate these effects and many more, so you must make sure you choose a decoder that can provide the lighting effects you want. Not all decoders let you program lighting effects on all of the function outputs, and some don't support any lighting effects.

A summary of each decoder's features is usually listed on the front of the package, but I'd recommend reading the decoder manual first. Most manuals are available at the manufacturer's Website.

To get the lighting function output to do something other than be on constantly, you must program CVs. The CV number and the CV value will vary between decoders. By programming the lighting effect CVs with different values, various effects can be achieved.

There is typically a CV for each function output. A list of values for each effect is in the decoder manual. In some cases, the flash rate or light intensity can be programmed.

Another thing to consider when choosing a decoder is the output current available on the function outputs. A single function output must be able to supply the current for all lights controlled by that function. Light bulbs can draw anywhere from 10mA to 100mA, and LEDs use between 5 and 20mA. Today's decoders can usually supply enough current for all but the biggest lighting jobs.

Most new locomotives use 1.5V bulbs. If the blue common wire is used,

Ditch lights (left) and rotary beacons (atop the Wisconsin Southern engine at right) are two locomotive lighting effects made possible with Digital Command Control. Mike Polsgrove explains how to add these features to your locomotive. *Bill Zuback*

a resistor is needed to drop the 12-14V of the function output to 1.5V for the bulb. If the +5V common is used with a 1.5V bulb, you'll need a smaller dropping resistor. Consult the decoder's manual for more information on selecting resistors.

Light-emitting diodes require a current-limiting resistor. The value of

the resistor can be calculated using the same method as for a voltage-dropping resistor. The forward voltage of an LED is typically between 2 and 3V.

Because of the differences in characteristics between light bulbs and LEDs, different CV values may be needed when programming lighting effects. Some decoder manufacturers recom-

mend not using LEDs at all.

Whether it's a Mars light, ditch lights, or rotary beacon, you can use DCC to add many realistic lighting effects to your locomotives. They not only make your locomotive look prototypical, but can enhance the realism of your next operating session.

Caboose lighting with DCC

Working caboose marker lights and interior lighting are examples of enhancing realism in rolling stock with DCC.

I had a Centralia Car Shops HO scale Soo Line caboose kit on my workbench, and I thought it would be nice to add interior lights and working marker lights controlled by a DCC decoder. The first task in lighting a caboose is to get the power from the rails into the car. If you're lucky, the caboose will already be set up for this. If not, you'll have to do it yourself either with pickup shoes or truck-mounted axle wipers that use the wheels to draw current from the rails.

Streamlined Backshop Services (www.sb4dcc.com) offers an assortment of axle wipers. I found the ones designed for Athearn trucks worked well on my Centralia model.

The brass axle wipers need to be formed per the instructions and placed between the truck and the caboose body. You must use metal wheelsets that conduct electricity from one wheel to the axle. The other wheel is insulated from the axle. Don't use wheelsets that have both wheels insulated from the axle. If you're unsure, check the wheelsets with multimeter on the resistance setting.

Each truck will only pick up power from one rail. It doesn't matter which rail is connected to which truck, but for each truck, both wheels must have the same side insulated. Solder a wire on each wiper prior to installing the wheels in the truck and mounting the truck to the caboose. Be sure to route the wires through the caboose floor first. I used one red wire and one black.

I wanted the interior lighting to simulate kerosene lanterns that were used in Soo Line wood cabooses. I consulted equipment diagrams and photos to determine the appropriate locations for the lamps in my caboose. I used dim yellow bulbs to simulate the prototype lamps.

I tested some Miniatronics 1.5V, 30mA lamps that I had handy. I used a 1.5V AA battery to test their brightness and see how they looked in the caboose before I wired them. In a brightly lit layout room the lamps only give a low glow, which was the effect I wanted. I also glued aluminum foil to the inside of the caboose's roof to reflect the light. Make sure the lights don't glow through the sides of the car.

Marker lights

According the 1962 Uniform Code of Operating Rules, the definition of a train is "An engine or more than one engine coupled, with or without cars, displaying markers." Sadly, none of my cabooses carried marker lights. To remedy this, I added Tomar markers with 1.5V bulbs (the firm also offers marker lights with LEDs).

A few companies make function-only decoders for projects like this. Each function output has a limited amount of current that it can supply, so I needed to know how much current my lights used. I already knew yellow bulbs drew 30mA each, but I needed to measure the Tomar markers. Again, the AA battery came in handy.

To measure the current the 1.5V bulb draws, place a multimeter (on the current setting) in series with the battery and the bulb. Most bulbs draw around 20-30mA.

I was a little surprised that the Tomar lights drew 45mA each. Most DCC decoders can easily handle that much current on a function output, but lowering the 12-14V typical for a decoder function output to 1.5V is more difficult when the bulb draws that much current.

The typical solution is to place a resistor in series with the bulb that, at a given current, drops enough voltage to safely light a 1.5V bulb. Ohm's Law is used to calculate the value of the resistor. Resistance = (Function voltage - bulb voltage / bulb current (mA)).

Using a function voltage of 14V and a 1.5V bulb that draws 45mA, the resistor value is (14-1.5)/.045, or 278Ω. The nearest standard value resistor is 330Ω. Generally you should use a resistor of a higher value than you calculate, otherwise the voltage on your bulb will be higher than 1.5V. Using a higher resistance will lower the voltage. This will make the lamp dimmer, but will also increase bulb life. A higher resistor value also allows for some variation in function voltage and the tolerance of the resistor values.

The power dissipated in the resistor must also be calculated using the formula: Power (watts) = (current)2 x (resistor value). In this case, it was (.045 x .045 x 330), or .67W.

You should always use a resistor of a higher power rating than the calculated value. The closer the actual power is to the power rating of the resistor, the hotter it will become. Thus, neither a ¼- or ½-watt resister would do in this case, and 1W resistors are very large. I could have used a number of half-watt resistors in series or parallel to split the power dissipated among several resistors. Also, I prefer the time-honored method of using two diodes in series and wiring them across the 1.5V bulb to make sure the voltage is always below 1.5. Since I had to do this for four different bulbs, the circuitry would have required a lot of space and generated a fair amount of heat, not good in an enclosed plastic caboose.

The option I finally chose was a Train Control Systems (TCS) 1.5V voltage regulator (TCS VR1.5), designed for lighting 1.5V bulbs.

The VR1.5 can only supply 120mA, and the sum of all my lighting was 150mA, which meant I needed two. A pair of VR1.5s are still smaller than the resistor network I would have needed. The VR1.5 can be used only with TCS decoders because, unlike other decoders, newer TCS decoders have a

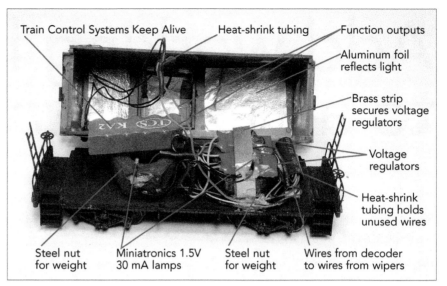

Careful planning is necessary so the decoder, voltage regulators, Keep Alive, and associated wiring will fit inside the caboose.

function ground wire that the voltage regulator needs. TCS makes the two-function FL2 and the four-function FL4. I used an FL4, but the FL2 would have worked.

Avoiding flickering

One drawback of lighted rolling stock is that the lights can flicker if the track is dirty or the car has dirty wheels. Another TCS product, Keep Alive, is designed to keep power on the decoder over dirty track. The manufacturer states that it will keep a locomotive running for 13-40 seconds without power, more than sufficient for the lighting alone. I used the KA2. Keep Alive can only be used with TCS decoders because of the extra ground wire.

Wiring the decoder, VR1.5s, and KA2 is pretty simple. I connected the black and red wires from the decoder to the black and red wires that I'd soldered to the axle wipers. The blue wire from the decoder is the function positive. I connected it to the blue wire of the VR1.5 and KA2. The black and white wire from the decoder is ground. It's connected to the black and white wires of the VR1.5 and KA2.

There are two tan wires from the VR1.5s. The wire from one VR1.5 goes to both marker lights; the wire from the other goes to both interior lights.

The decoder's brown and pink wires are the function outputs (when they're on, they're "ground"). The F3 and F4

function buttons of a DCC throttle control these by default. The decoder can be remapped to control them by other function buttons if you desire. Function output wires are the negative wire. I connected the decoder's brown wire to the other side of the interior lights, and the decoder's pink wire to the other side of the marker lights. Then I soldered all of the connections and covered them with heat-shrink tubing.

Since I only needed to turn lights on and off, no decoder programming was required other than setting the address. I used 9091 for the decoder.

I suggest testing the wiring with other bulbs before connecting them to the bulbs within the marker lights. If the lights are miswired, it's expensive and difficult to replace the markers.

I used double-sided foam tape to attach the decoder to the floor of the caboose, and a larger piece of heat-shrink tubing to contain the unused decoder wires. I also used double-sided tape to attach the KA2 to one of the large nuts that I used as weights.

The two VR1.5s got a little warm, so I fashioned a bracket out of a strip of brass and used it to hold down the VR1.5s. The metal nut will help dissipate the heat from the VR1.5s. I epoxied the brass bracket to the sides of the nut.

Adding this lighting took some careful planning and wiring, but the end results were worth the time.

Add working lights to a bi-level cab coach

The marker lights, headlights, and rotary beacon on this Kato HO scale bi-level commuter cab coach can all be controlled using Digital Command Control.

A recent visit to a friend's HO scale Chicago & North Western layout set in the railroad's namesake city inspired me to try my hand at adding DCC lighting effects to a bi-level cab coach.

For those not familiar with Chicago's push-pull commuter operation, inbound trains (those toward the city) are pushed by the locomotive but controlled by an engineer in the cab coach. There is a small control cab on the second level of the car that allows the engineer to operate the locomotive on the other end of the train. On the outbound trip, the locomotive is in the lead and the cab coach displays the marker lights.

I chose the Kato bi-level car over other HO scale models because the firm offers an interior lighting kit that's DCC compatible. I used the kit as-is and decided not to control it with the decoder. I used the Train Control Systems (TCS) FL4 light-only decoder for the headlights, rotary beacon, and marker lights.

The Kato cab coach lighting is designed for direct-current operation. When the cab is leading, the headlight is on. When the car is trailing, the marker lights are illuminated. The rotary beacon is a non-functioning detail part.

There is a light board in the cab end of the car with two light-emitting diodes (LEDs), **1**. The tall one sticks up into the cab interior where it illuminates a clear plastic rod to the headlights. The short LED lights a separate rod for the markers.

Disassembly

I had to completely disassemble the car to wire it for DCC. Removing the interior seating was easy. However, I had to remove the marker lights and extract the light pipes to get into the cab interior.

The rotary beacon isn't factory installed, so I planned on drilling a hole in the roof to mount it. The underside of the translucent beacon would then be exposed to the car's interior, allowing me to mount an LED to illuminate it.

However, I discovered that the light rod for the headlights would interfere with this. After careful measuring and filing, I mounted a 3mm ultra bright LED from Miniatronics on top of the headlight rod. I used a piece of electrical tape to prevent the LED's glow from entering the headlight rod, **2**.

Manufacturers of LEDs mark the anode and cathode differently, but I found that it's sometimes easier to use a 12V power supply (like an old DC throttle) and a 330Ω resistor to determine which is which. I quickly connect the resistor in series with the LED. When the LED illuminates, the lead connected to the positive side of the power supply is the anode.

I soldered the blue wire to the anode (positive) side of the LED for the rotary beacon, and a green wire to the cathode (negative). I covered the exposed leads with heat-shrink tubing and fed the wires down the same hole past the headlight pipe that the tall LED fits into, **3**.

Once I was satisfied with how the beacon worked, I turned my attention to the light board. There are two long brass contacts that supply rail power to the light board. A small brass contact provides power for the LEDs.

As wired for DC operation, a single current-limiting resistor is used for both LEDs. The cathode of one diode is wired to the anode of the other. This allows current in one direction to illuminate one LED and current in the other direction to light the other.

To control the headlights and marker lights with DCC, the anodes of both LEDs must be connected to the blue wire, **4**. To do this, I removed the tall LED and reinstalled it backward. I then used a hobby knife to cut the printed-circuit (PC) board trace between what is now the cathode of the tall LED to isolate it from the cathode of the short LED. This is the trace connected to the surface-mount resistor. The resistor must also be isolated from the long brass strips. Check the cuts with an ohmmeter to make sure there's no contact.

Decoder mounting, final wiring

I mounted the TCS decoder between the lower level seats, **5**. Once I figured out how much wire I'd need for each function, I trimmed the excess from the decoder. I soldered the blue wire to the common anode terminal of the LEDs, the red and black wires to the brass rail contacts individually, and the violet

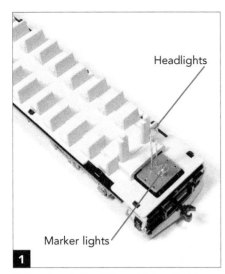

1

This printed-circuit board is located in the cab end of the gallery bi-level car. The light board has a tall-mounted LED for the headlights and a short LED for the marker lights.

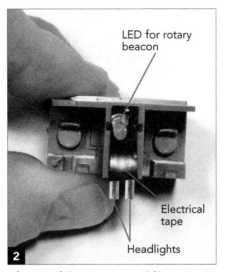

2

After careful measuring and filing, Mike was able to seat the LED for the rotary beacon on top of the clear plastic headlight rod. The electrical tape prevents the glow of the LED from appearing in the headlights.

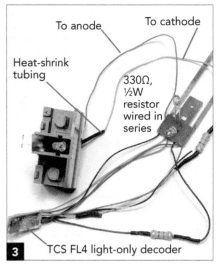

3

After determining the anode and cathode leads, Mike wired the LED to the printed-circuit board. He covered the exposed leads with heat-shrink tubing to prevent short circuits.

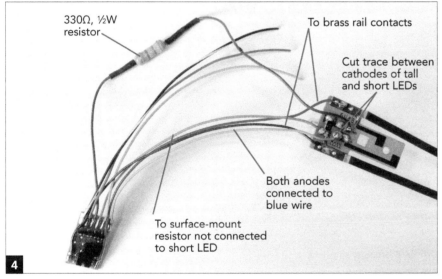

4

Both anodes of the headlight and marker light LEDs must be connected to the blue decoder wire. Mike used a hobby knife to cut the trace between the cathodes of the tall and short LEDs.

5

Mike set the decoder and wires in the lowest level of the car. He used electrical tape to hold the decoder in place.

wire to the side of the surface-mount resistor not connected to the red LED. The tall LED now needed its own current-limiting resistor, so I soldered a 330Ω, ½-watt resistor in series with the brown wire.

At this point I double-checked my connections and made sure the rail contacts weren't connected to anything except the red and black wires. I also made sure that the cathodes of the LEDs were separated.

Then I checked the wiring by con-

necting leads from my test track to the brass contacts. The TCS decoder is programmed to address 3. The violet wire is controlled by F2 on the DCC throttle, and the brown wire by F3. I was able to turn the lights on and off with my throttle, so I was ready to wire the diode for the rotary beacon.

I connected the LED's leads to the blue and green wires and used another 330Ω, ½W resistor in series with the green wire. After testing the beacon, I programmed CV51 to 38 to activate

the LED's simulated rotary lighting effect.

I reassembled the car, discarding the on/off switch on the bottom of the light board. I tested the model, making sure the functions worked properly (F1 for the rotating beacon, F2 for the marker lights, and F3 for the headlight). The finished car looks great and will add realism to my friend's push-pull commuter service.

Light passenger car interiors with DCC

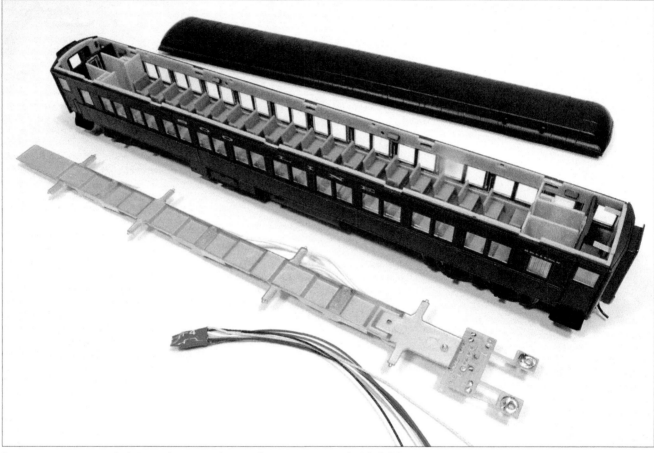

Passenger car interior lighting enhances realism and is easy to control with DCC.

If you have a direct-current (DC) model railroad, you've probably struggled to provide constant lighting for your passenger cars. Since the track voltage controls train speed in DC, when your train is stopped at the station, the passengers are left in the dark.

DCC provides a constant track voltage. This means that whether your train is making a station stop or rolling down the tracks, the interior lighting will remain at the same brightness. However, you must take into account the extra load of the lights when calculating the size of your DCC booster, as it supplies all the power for them.

Here's how I added DCC-operated interior lighting to a Walthers heavyweight passenger car. The techniques can be easily adapted for use in cars by other manufacturers.

Most of today's passenger cars are equipped with electrical contacts for interior lighting. If your model doesn't have contacts, you can modify most plastic trucks by adding metal wheelsets and simple pickup wipers or shoes (see the section on caboose lighting, page 80, for information on wipers).

Track voltage provided by a booster varies depending on the system, but most DCC systems range from 12-16 volts (V).

Light bulbs will operate on either DC or the AC signal of a DCC system. If you use an 18V bulb connected directly across the rails, you'll likely be happy with the results.

An alternative is to use a low-voltage bulb with a dropping resistor. Calculating the value of the resistor is the same as for a locomotive headlight or caboose markers (see page 83).

Light-emitting diodes (LEDs) may also be used to light passenger car interiors, but they won't operate on AC. Though the LED will rectify the AC signal into a DC signal, DCC voltage often exceeds the diode's Peak-Inverse-Voltage (PIV). To prevent the DCC voltage from exceeding the PIV, use a bridge rectifier and a current-limiting resistor.

Walthers passenger cars come equipped with factory-installed electrical pickups, and the firm sells separate lighting kits for both DC and DCC. The kits are easy to install—just remove the roof and set the light bar in place.

The DC kit (933-1087) uses a 5V regulator to lower the voltage. This provides constant lighting if the track voltage is above 6V.

The DCC version (933-1088) uses three bulbs in series so they equally divide the voltage. On a typical 14V DCC system, each bulb operates on a little less than 5V.

I had several Walthers coaches to equip with interior lighting, so I purchased the DCC lighting kits. I also wanted the ability to turn the lights on and off, so I added a DCC decoder to each car. I chose a Digitrax TF4 function-only decoder because it's compact and has four function outputs. Train Control Systems (TCS) also makes lighting-only decoders, however, you can use just about any decoder that has function outputs.

Decoder installation
The Walthers light bar has two rivets that make contact with copper strips at one end to provide track power to the top of the car, **1**. A small printed-circuit (PC) board connects the lights in series.

To start, I removed all the bulb wires from the PC board. I then soldered one wire from each bulb to an unused section of the PC board. (See **1**.) The Digitrax decoder's blue wire is the lighting common. I soldered the blue wire to the PC board as well, connecting it to the three bulb wires already there.

Next, I soldered the red and black decoder wires to the wires from the PC board's contact rivets, also shown in **1**.

In order to properly illuminate the bulbs with a decoder output on my DCC system, I needed to drop the voltage about 7V. The function-output voltage can be measured directly with a DC voltmeter when the decoder is connected to the track and the function

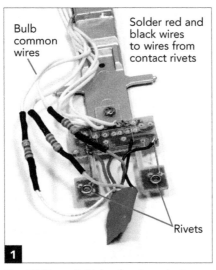

1

The Walthers light bar has two rivets that make contact with copper strips to provide track power to the top of the car. Mike soldered the red and black decoder wires to the wires from the PC board's contact rivets.

is turned on. The blue wire is positive and the function outputs are negative.

I also measured the current each bulb drew by placing a multimeter in series with the bulbs and powering it from a DC power pack set to 12V. The Walthers bulbs draw about 30mA. When choosing a decoder, make sure the function outputs can provide the necessary current for your bulbs.

Using Ohm's Law, I calculated that in order to drop 7V at 30mA, I needed about a 250Ω (7/.030) resistor. My original calculation of the bulb voltage was based on a 14V DCC system. I figured that the bulbs were capable of handling a few more volts than I'd calculated, so I used 220Ω resistors. I did one more calculation before applying the power.

To prevent the resistor from burning up, the power (watt) rating must be above the calculated power. To calculate power, square the current and multiply the result by the resistor value: here, (.030 x .030) x 220 = .198, or approximately 200mW. Since that's less than 250mW (¼W), it was safe to use the resistor. Be aware that the closer the working power is to the rated power, the hotter the resistor will get. As a precaution, I mounted the resistors so they wouldn't contact any plastic parts of the model.

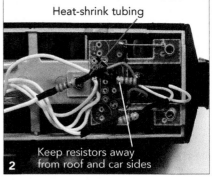

2

After successfully testing the light bar, Mike installed it and reassembled the passenger car. He covered any bare wires with heat-shrink tubing to prevent a short circuit.

Finishing and programming
From the factory, white is the function 1 (F1) wire, yellow is F2, green is F3, and violet is F4. I soldered 220Ω dropping resistors to the white, yellow, and green wires and covered the connections with shrink tubing, **2**. (Don't cover the resistor itself!) I soldered the other side of the resistors to the open wires on the bulbs, and I covered those connections with shrink tubing as well. I then trimmed off the decoder's unneeded violet wire (F4).

I tested my wiring by connecting the rivets directly to the track with test clips. If you want different functions to control the lighting, the Digitrax TF4 offers function mapping, which allows you to change the button controls assigned to each function output.

After successfully testing the wiring, I installed the light bar and reassembled the passenger car. Since my passenger trains maintain their consists throughout the course of an operating session, I programmed the decoder's address to the train number. This allows me to turn all of the train's lighting on with one address. If cars in your passenger train are switched during a session, you may want to program the decoder's address to the car number.

Adding interior lighting is a great way to enhance the realism of passenger cars and show off those well-detailed interiors. Though installing the lights isn't necessarily difficult, you should work carefully and double-check your wiring along the way.

Controlling train-order signals

Mike uses DCC decoders and an NCE Mini Panel to operate the train-order signals on his HO scale Soo Line layout.

Since my HO Soo Line layout is set in 1963 and operations are controlled by timetable and train orders, I needed signals at each train-order station. On the prototype, these signals were controlled by the operator in the depot or tower. On model railroads, many layout owners have signals controlled from a central location by an operator or dispatcher. I planned to have the signals controlled by the dispatcher. However, I wasn't thrilled about running wires from each depot to the dispatcher's desk, so I wired the signals with DCC.

I chose a Digitrax TF4 function-only decoder for the signals. The mobile decoder lacks motor control, but it can be used to operate up to four lights. With three lights in each direction to illuminate, I used three functions of the decoder. There are eastbound and westbound signals on the same mast, so two decoders are required.

I couldn't find any commercial signals similar to the Soo's. At the recommendation of a friend, I contacted Randy Piccuilla at Custom Signal Systems (www.customsignalsystems. com), and he made my signals. He used colored LEDs for the aspects.

The LEDs are wired with magnet wire. This fine-gauge wire is coated with varnish insulation and is small enough to fit through the signal mast to the underside of the benchwork.

Sub-panels

I try to build sub-panels whenever I can. This allows me to complete most of the wiring at my workbench and simply connect the panels to the layout wiring.

For the train-order signals, I used a scrap piece of pressboard (a type of hardboard). I attached a 12-position barrier strip to the board to make the

connections between the circuitry on the subpanel and the wires under the layout. I used double-sided foam tape to mount the decoders, **1**.

The LEDs require current-limiting resistors. I used $1K\Omega$ resistors and a piece of perforated project board to mount them.

Both decoders are wired identically. The red, black, and blue wires are connected directly to terminals on the barrier strip. The other wires are connected to one side of each resistor. The default function mapping of the TF4 is that the white wire is controlled by function (F) 1 on a DCC throttle, the yellow wire by F2, the green wire by F3, and the purple wire by F4. In this case, the purple wire is unused and not connected.

After I wired the panel, I programmed the decoders. The westbound signal is programmed to the station's milepost with the number 1 appended. The eastbound signal has the number 2 appended.

I mounted the panel under the layout and connected it to the signals and track power. I connected the red and black wires to the track power. Each blue wire from the decoder is attached to the common anode wire of the signal it controls. I connected the white wire's resistor to the signal wire connected to the green LED. This allows F1 to control the green LED. Then I connected the yellow wire's resistor to the yellow diode. The resistor connected to the green wire is attached to the red diode.

Control panel

At this point, a DCC throttle can control the signals. However, I wanted a control panel with toggle switches. I'd previously used the NCE Mini Panel to control the turnouts in one of my staging yards. I planned on using a Mini

Panel to control a staging yard that's next to my dispatcher's desk. The panel has plenty of inputs for both, so I wired my train-order signal control panel to the inputs of the NCE Mini Panel.

The Mini Panel has 31 inputs and is designed for creating control panels and other control functions. When an input is grounded, a series of DCC commands are sent through the NCE cab bus to the command station and then out the power booster to the track. Since I used mobile decoders, I needed to send locomotive commands.

The Mini Panel is capable of sending locomotive and stationary decoder commands. It uses the NCE cab bus to send commands to the command station, so it can only be used with an NCE system.

In addition to hardwired control panel solutions, there are a number of computer programs like the free Panel-Pro from JMRI that could be used (jmri.sourceforge.net/help/en/html/apps/PanelPro/PanelPro.shtml). You need an interface between a computer and your DCC system to use these.

To build my panel, I used a double-pole double-throw (DPDT) center-off switch to control each signal head (one for the eastbound signal and one for the westbound signal). I used one pole of the DPDT switch for the green and red indicators. I wired the center terminal to ground and each of the other terminals to separate inputs. I used red wire for the red signal input and green wire for the green signal input. Color-coding makes troubleshooting easier, **2**.

When the switch is thrown in one direction, the red input is grounded. When the switch is thrown in the other direction, the green input is grounded. The yellow input is a little more complicated. I wanted one switch to control all three signal aspects, so the center off position must ground the yellow input. Being an off position, there is no connection made when the toggle switch is in the center. The team at NCE recommended a nifty little circuit consisting of an unused input and a single NPN transistor, **3**. I used the RadioShack no. 276-2058 transistor.

The NPN transistors have three terminals: a base, an emitter, and a col-

Mike did most of the wiring for his signals at the workbench. By building this sub-panel, he limited the amount of under-the-layout wiring.

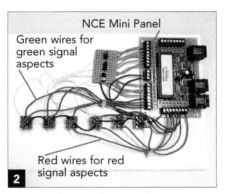

Mike used red and green wires to coordinate with the color of the signal aspects. This makes troubleshooting easier.

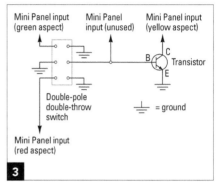

In this circuit, the transistor grounds the yellow input (turning the yellow aspect on) when the switch is in the center-off position.

lector. A diagram on the box identifies the terminals. The other pole of the toggle has the center terminal connected to the base of the transistor. The other two terminals are connected to the ground on the switch. The base of the transistor is also connected to an unused input of the Mini Panel.

The collector is attached to another input, and the emitter is connected to the ground of the Mini Panel. Each yellow signal light uses two inputs, one of which is programmed.

With the Mini Panel wired, I programmed each input individually with NCE's ProCab. When an input is grounded, the Mini Panel executes a sequence of four commands. Inputs can be linked together to increase the number of commands.

Input no. 1 is the yellow aspect of the westbound Marshfield signal, so the program consisted of two steps. The first command is to select the mobile (locomotive) decoder, in this case 2811. The second command was

to turn on function F2. The function command controls four functions at a time, so I made sure the green (F1) and the red (F3) functions were off.

Input no. 13 is the green aspect of the westbound Marshfield signal. The first command in the sequence is to again select locomotive decoder 2811. The second command is to turn on function F1. I programmed all other inputs the same way.

At this point, all I had to do was mount the control panel and connect it permanently to the NCE cab bus. Other than connecting the decoder sub-panel to the signal and connecting the Mini Panel the cab bus, there was no under-the-layout wiring. Additional signals can be added at any time just by tying them in to the track bus.

Functioning train-control signals add another element of realism to operating sessions. If you use a mobile decoder, such as the Digitrax TF4, make sure your control panel is capable of issuing locomotive commands.

Lightning Source UK Ltd.
Milton Keynes UK
UKOW07f2338161117
312853UK00002B/22/P

9 780890 249826